DETROIT PUBLIC LIBRARY

W9-BXE-082

Simple Computer
Tune-up

AUG 2007

DUFFIELD BRANCH LIBRARY
2507 W. GRAND BLVD.
DETROIT, MI 48208-1236
(313) 224-6456

0 45601581

Simple Computer Tune-up:
Speed Up Your PC

CA
with Eric Geier and Jim Geier

Wiley Publishing, Inc.

Simple Computer Tune-up: Speed Up Your PC

Published by
Wiley Publishing, Inc.
10475 Crosspoint Boulevard
Indianapolis, IN 46256
www.wiley.com

Copyright © 2007 by Wiley Publishing, Inc., Indianapolis, Indiana

Published simultaneously in Canada

ISBN: 978-0-470-06855-7

Manufactured in the United States of America

10 9 8 7 6 5 4 3 2 1

1B/QU/QR/QX/IN

No part of this publication may be reproduced, stored in a retrieval system or transmitted in any form or by any means, electronic, mechanical, photocopying, recording, scanning or otherwise, except as permitted under Sections 107 or 108 of the 1976 United States Copyright Act, without either the prior written permission of the Publisher, or authorization through payment of the appropriate per-copy fee to the Copyright Clearance Center, 222 Rosewood Drive, Danvers, MA 01923, (978) 750-8400, fax (978) 646-8600. Requests to the Publisher for permission should be addressed to the Legal Department, Wiley Publishing, Inc., 10475 Crosspoint Blvd., Indianapolis, IN 46256, (317) 572-3447, fax (317) 572-4355, or online at http://www.wiley.com/go/permissions.

LIMIT OF LIABILITY/DISCLAIMER OF WARRANTY: THE PUBLISHER AND THE AUTHOR MAKE NO REPRESENTATIONS OR WARRANTIES WITH RESPECT TO THE ACCURACY OR COMPLETENESS OF THE CONTENTS OF THIS WORK AND SPECIF-ICALLY DISCLAIM ALL WARRANTIES, INCLUDING WITHOUT LIMITATION WAR-RANTIES OF FITNESS FOR A PARTICULAR PURPOSE. NO WARRANTY MAY BE CREATED OR EXTENDED BY SALES OR PROMOTIONAL MATERIALS. THE ADVICE AND STRATEGIES CONTAINED HEREIN MAY NOT BE SUITABLE FOR EVERY SIT-UATION. THIS WORK IS SOLD WITH THE UNDERSTANDING THAT THE PUB-LISHER IS NOT ENGAGED IN RENDERING LEGAL, ACCOUNTING, OR OTHER PROFESSIONAL SERVICES. IF PROFESSIONAL ASSISTANCE IS REQUIRED, THE SERVICES OF A COMPETENT PROFESSIONAL PERSON SHOULD BE SOUGHT. NEITHER THE PUBLISHER NOR THE AUTHOR SHALL BE LIABLE FOR DAMAGES ARISING HEREFROM. THE FACT THAT AN ORGANIZATION OR WEBSITE IS REFERRED TO IN THIS WORK AS A CITATION AND/OR A POTENTIAL SOURCE OF FURTHER INFORMATION DOES NOT MEAN THAT THE AUTHOR OR THE PUB-LISHER ENDORSES THE INFORMATION THE ORGANIZATION OR WEBSITE MAY PROVIDE OR RECOMMENDATIONS IT MAY MAKE. FURTHER, READERS SHOULD BE AWARE THAT INTERNET WEBSITES LISTED IN THIS WORK MAY HAVE CHANGED OR DISAPPEARED BETWEEN WHEN THIS WORK WAS WRITTEN AND WHEN IT IS READ.

For general information on our other products and services or to obtain technical support, please contact our Customer Care Department within the U.S. at (800) 762-2974, outside the U.S. at (317) 572-3993 or fax (317) 572-4002.

Library of Congress Control Number: Available from the publisher.

Trademarks: Wiley, the Wiley logo, and related trade dress are trademarks or registered trademarks of John Wiley & Sons, Inc. and/or its affiliates, in the United States and other countries, and may not be used without written permission. The CA logo and related CA trademarks are trademarks or registered trademarks of CA International, Inc. All other trademarks are the property of their respective owners. Wiley Publishing, Inc., is not associated with any product or vendor mentioned in this book.

Wiley also publishes its books in a variety of electronic formats. Some content that appears in print may not be available in electronic books.

Credits

Executive Editor
Carol Long

Senior Development Editor
Tom Dinse

Production Editor
William A. Barton

Copy Editor
Kim Cofer

Editorial Manager
Mary Beth Wakefield

Production Manager
Tim Tate

**Vice President and
Executive Group Publisher**
Richard Swadley

**Vice President and
Executive Publisher**
Joseph B. Wikert

Project Coordinator
Erin Smith

**Graphics and Production
Specialists**
Erin Zeltner

Quality Control Technician
Brian H. Walls

Proofreading and Indexing
Techbooks

Anniversary Logo Design
Richard Pacifico

Contents

Acknowledgments

CA would like to thank all of the people who have contributed their technical, editorial, administrative, and/or creative expertise to the making of its first series of CA Simple computer solution books.

Laural Gentry

Diana Gruhn

Lawrence Guerin

Mark Haswell

Robyn Herbert

Christopher Hickey

George Kafkarkou

David Luft

Gary McGuire

Stefana Ribaudo-Muller

Introduction

As more and more software becomes available and computers increase in complexity, problems with performance are certain to arise. If your PC is misbehaving, don't let it ruin your day. This book explains how to make the best out of your PC by using PC Pitstop Optimize, which cures many PC "sicknesses" without the need for upgrading or replacing your existing PC. As bonus material, this book also includes loads of information that will help you troubleshoot more serious problems and even add new capabilities to your computer.

How This Book Is Organized

This book is organized in a very simple manner and is summed up by the following:

- First you can learn about the problems.

- Then you can learn about the solutions to combat those problems.

- Next you'll prepare to implement the solutions.

- Then the book will help you properly employ the solutions with step-by-step directions, illustrations, and tips.

Part 1: Understanding the Issues and Solutions

The chapters in this part of the book will help you understand the issues relating to PC performance and you'll be introduced to solutions to fix the issues. This part of the book is a good place to start before actually optimizing and using the included software, PC Pitstop Optimize.

Chapter 1: This chapter discusses the major causes of poor PC performance, such as "junk files" and other not so obvious contributors. In later chapters, after learning this background information, you'll be shown exactly how to overcome these types of problems.

Chapter 2: PC Pitstop Optimize scans and identifies many common problems that plague most computers—get a better performing computer without the expense or difficulty of adding new hardware.

Part 2: Optimizing Your PC

This part of the book gives you step-by-step instructions on how to optimize your PC to ensure your computer operates at its full potential. We walk you through the installation of the included software, PC Pitstop Optimize, which addresses many issues related to poor and degraded PC performance. In addition, you'll learn many other tasks you can perform to ensure that you get the most out of your PC.

Chapter 3: Installing PC Pitstop Optimize is the first step toward quickly and easily resolving many common computing issues that your PC may be currently experiencing in order to improve the performance and stability of your computer.

Chapter 4: Before PC Pitstop Optimize can do any optimization it first needs to scan your PC for junk files, invalid system and Internet settings, and other items that should be addressed to ensure maximum PC performance. Then you'll have the chance to specify exactly which items are removed or changed.

Chapter 5: This chapter shows how to easily initiate and complete an optimization on your PC.

Chapter 6: This chapter shows how to perform many tasks that will help optimize your PC. Performing these additional tasks, along with using PC Pitstop Optimize regularly or at least once a month, will ensure your PC runs faster and more efficiently.

Chapter 7: To ensure you get the most out of PC Pitstop Optimize you should keep the software up-to-date with any fixes or new features, which may include updates to the files and system settings it uses to optimize your PC. Therefore, before each use you should check for updates.

Chapter 8: This chapter discusses common problems and fixes you may experience when using PC Pitstop Optimize and also lets you know where you can get more help.

Part 3: Bonus Material

The chapters in this part contain additional tips when dealing with an older PC, which is likely the reason you are using PC Pitstop Optimize. For example, upgrading your PC can be very useful for maximizing your current computer's performance. Therefore, we discuss upgrading and show you how to perform many common upgrades, such as installing more memory.

These bonus chapters save you lots of money by avoiding the need to purchase separate books on these topics. We just want to be sure that you get the best out of your PC!

Chapter 9: Although Windows XP is arguably the most stable and reliable version of Windows thus far it isn't perfect. Occasionally you might hit a few digital potholes that throw XP out of alignment. To ensure a smooth ride and eliminate common XP problems, follow the tips in this chapter.

Chapter 10: Certain features of Windows XP may not be set to your liking. To customize Windows to meet your personal preferences, follow the tips in this chapter.

Chapter 11: From connection difficulties to broken downloads, Internet issues are some of the most common problems. Learn the secrets of the pros by following the tips in this chapter.

Chapter 12: Before upgrading your hardware, installing new software, or troubleshooting a computer problem, you need to know certain things about your PC—such as what version of Windows or how much RAM you have. Regardless of whether you tackle the computer work yourself or hire certified professionals, an analysis of your computer is the logical starting point.

Chapter 13: A computer has many removable parts that can be replaced or upgraded to provide extra speed, power, or storage. This chapter shows why and how to upgrade your PC to make better use of it.

Chapter 14: Half the fun of using a computer comes from its accessories (usually referred to as "peripherals") such as printers, scanners, and digital cameras. This chapter explains how to install and set up common peripherals and provides fixes for problems you might run into.

Chapter 15: Let's face it: Sometimes computers can be so frustrating that they make you want to abandon them forever and switch to an old-fashioned, reliable typewriter. But before you take such a drastic action, scan through this chapter to learn how to troubleshoot and solve common PC problems.

Chapter 16: Buying a computer is a lot like buying a car. Both require you to research the numerous makes and models available and carefully select the features—and price tag—that are right for you. This chapter explains how to go about buying a computer in a way that best satisfies your needs.

Who Should Read This Book

Anyone who uses the Internet, email, or a computer should read this book.

Whether you are a self-proclaimed computer illiterate or a life-long IT professional, this book will give you the tools and understanding to free your computer of clutter and optimize your PC so it can operate at its fullest potential.

What's on the CD-ROM

This book comes bundled with a CD containing PC Pitstop Optimize, which scans and identifies many common problems that plague most computers. PC Pitstop Optimize allows you to improve the performance of your computer without the expense or difficulty of adding new hardware.

PC Pitstop Optimize will help with the following:

- Energize Internet speeds
- Recoup system resources
- Maximize hard drive space
- Eliminate registry errors
- Revitalize system performance

Part 1

UNDERSTAND THE ISSUES AND SOLUTIONS

In This Part

Chapter 1: Causes of Poor PC Performance

Chapter 2: Understanding PC Pitstop Optimize

The chapters in this part of the book will help you understand the issues relating to PC performance, such as the causes of your computer's poor or degraded performance. You'll also be introduced to solutions that address these issues, which allow you to perform some simple optimizations that will make your computing experience faster and better.

This part of the book is a good place to start before actually optimizing and using the included software, PC Pitstop Optimize.

CAUSES OF POOR PC PERFORMANCE

This chapter discusses the major causes of poor PC performance, such as "junk files" and other not so obvious contributors. In later chapters, after learning this background information, you'll be shown exactly how to overcome these types of problems.

Temporary Files

Computers naturally create many different temporary files, which are typically stored for your advantage. However, these temporary files on your computer (as the following sections discuss) can stack up, which can contribute to poor PC performance.

Internet Cache

Web browsers (for example Internet Explorer) typically create temporary files, often referred to as Internet Cache, during web browsing. These temporary files usually aren't needed after you are finished surfing the web, and can take up large amounts of space on your hard drive. Therefore these files, if not removed periodically, may contribute to poor PC performance.

If you are curious, you can view Internet Explorer's cache:

1. Open Internet Explorer.
2. Open Internet Options from the Tools menu, as shown in Figure 1-1.

Figure 1-1: Opening Internet Options

3. Click Settings... under the Temporary Internet Files section, as pointed out in Figure 1-2.

Figure 1-2: Accessing the temporary Internet files settings

4. Click View Files..., as seen in Figure 1-3.

The Temporary Internet Files window will appear, as Figure 1-3 shows.

Figure 1-3: Viewing temporary Internet files

Recycle Bin

Remember, files are not actually removed from the hard drive when you delete them the first time. For instance, deleting files for the first time actually sends them to the Recycle Bin. Then from there you can either permanently remove them from your computer, or in case you figured out that they should not have been deleted, you can restore them.

You can easily view the content of your Recycle Bin:

1. Go to your desktop.

2. Double-click the Recycle Bin, as shown in Figure 1-4.

Figure 1-4: Opening the Recycle Bin

3. The Recycle Bin will appear, as shown in Figure 1-5.

Windows Temporary Files

The Windows operating system and other applications create temporary files for various reasons, such as during software installations.

These temporary files, however, are typically not needed after the application exits or when Windows is shut down. In many cases, the applications do not always clean up after themselves and leave behind a stack of files, which will use up some of your computer's valuable disk space.

Figure 1-5: The Recycle Bin

Getting Out of Date

Microsoft releases periodic updates for Windows to ensure your PC is protected from the latest known security holes and programming bugs or errors. In addition, many of these updates will help increase your PC's performance.

Therefore you shouldn't let Windows get out of date; otherwise you'll compromise the security and performance of your PC.

Unused Files and Programs

Unused programs and files are one of the biggest contributors to wasted disk space and can cause a reduction in your PC's perform-ance. As a general rule of thumb, the less disk space you use of your hard drive, the better overall PC performance you'll experience.

Therefore, it's best to remove software programs that aren't used and files that you don't need anymore.

Unnecessary Startup Programs

Many software programs may add themselves (with or without your knowledge) to your Startup folder, which may cause your PC to take longer to start up.

Additionally, these programs running in the background will steal computing power from other applications you are using and will overall bog down your PC.

Invalid Registry Entries

The registry contains information that Windows continually references during operation, such as profiles for each user, the applications installed on the computer and the types of documents that each can create, property sheet settings for folders and application icons, what hardware exists on the system, and the ports that are being used.

There are many specific registry keys that can slow a computer's performance. These are typically invalid keys containing information about COM and ActiveX objects. These objects are parts of programs, and when you remove the programs, these keys sometimes still exist. However, if these registry keys aren't removed they can contribute to slower PC performance.

Here are some common areas of the registry that may contain invalid keys:

- Invalid Class IDs (CLSID)
- Invalid Program Identifiers (ProgID)
- Invalid Type Libraries (TypeLib)
- Invalid Interfaces

Hard Drive Errors

Data in hard drives can become corrupt and contain errors, such as from the following situations:

- Improper shutdown from power outage
- Power surges
- PC suddenly resets (bad power connection or supply)
- PC crashes or locks up, so that shutdown is impossible

When there are errors in a hard drive, it can't work at its optimum performance. Typically, hard drive errors won't be noticeable to the PC user, which makes the situation even worse.

Fragmentation

Fragmentation is the condition in which files are divided into pieces scattered around a hard drive and can have a significant impact on PC performance. This is because it takes more time to access files on a hard drive if they are fragmented.

The following are causes of fragmentation:

- Installing software
- Uninstalling software
- Moving files
- Deleting files

Even though fragmentation is common and occurs naturally, there are ways to help the problem, which are discussed in a later chapter.

2

UNDERSTANDING PC PITSTOP OPTIMIZE

PC Pitstop Optimize scans and identifies many common problems that plague most computers — get a better performing computer without the expense or difficulty of adding new hardware.

General Information

CA has teamed up with PCPitstop.com, a leading online computing diagnostic and optimization destination, to offer a very exciting product to CA customers.

Since PC Pitstop opened in March 2000, it has tested and optimized more than a million computers. During that time, it has taken the experience from the services offered on its website and created an application that makes your PC run faster, allows it to be more stable, and cleans up hard drive space.

PC Pitstop has designed the Optimize program to be easy to use and resolve many common computing issues that you may be currently experiencing.

PC Pitstop Optimize can improve the performance and stability of just about any PC running Windows XP, 2000, ME, or 98.

Why Choose PC Pitstop Optimize?

There are many reasons to choose PC Pitstop Optimize, such as:

- **It's developed by a trusted company**

  Since PC Pitstop opened in March 2000, it has tested and optimized more than a million computers.

- **It's backed by CA**

  Given that CA, which provides software to 98% of the Fortune 500 companies, teamed with PC Pitstop shows an extreme level of confidence.

- **It's powerful technology**

  PC Pitstop developed its technology to be flexible yet powerful, which can be used to improve many of today's common web and computing experiences.

PC Pitstop Optimize Features

The following are several features of PC Pitstop Optimize:

- **Energize Internet Speeds**

  Improve your Internet connection up to 200% by adjusting your Windows Internet settings, based on your connection type.

- **Recoup System Resources**

  Eliminate unnecessary background processes and get back memory and processor cycles stolen by rogue applications.

- **Maximize Hard Drive Space**

  Quickly and easily find and remove unnecessary files, making your drive run even faster.

- **Eliminate Registry Errors**

  Remove erroneous and leftover registry entries created by viruses, spyware, and incorrect program removal.

- **Revitalize System Performance**

  Increase your system performance by tweaking Windows settings.

New Features in Version 1.5

The new version of PC Pitstop Optimize, which is included with this book, doubles the performance tweak from the previous versions by adding things such as:

- Fresh new look
- Scheduling options
- Automatic updates

- More registry tweaks
- Enhanced Internet optimization
- Internet download and ping tests
- Removal of unneeded programs running in background
- Clean up of broken add/remove program entries
- Deleting unnecessary files across multiple users

Frequently Asked Questions

This section contains a few common questions and answers relating to PC Pitstop Optimize.

Can I Undo the Changes It Makes?

The hard disk clean-up permanently removes unnecessary files and cannot be undone. However, all of the other utilities in Optimize can be completely reversed. The very first action Optimize does before making any registry setting changes is to make a backup of these settings. When you run Optimize it will give you the option to restore the registry settings back to any point before the application was run.

What Files Does It Delete?

Windows often forgets to clean up many files that are no longer needed by the system. The space taken up by these files can clog your disk and cause slower disk access. These files are in three major categories:

- **Recycle Bin**

  Files are not actually removed from the drive when you initially delete them. Instead, the files are moved to the Recycle Bin where you can retrieve them if you later decide that you should not have deleted them. Optimize empties your Recycle Bin to reclaim this disk space.

- **Internet Cache**

  Internet Explorer (IE) creates temporary files that are not needed after you finish surfing. These files can take up large amounts of space and should be removed periodically. Although you can clear the cache in IE, Optimize uses a more thorough method that deletes files left behind by IE.

- **Temporary Files**

  Windows and applications create various temporary files that are not needed after the application exits or Windows is shut down. In many cases, however, the applications do not always clean up after themselves.

After scanning your system, Optimize gives you the option to review the files that it found and to select which files should be deleted.

What System Settings Does It Change?

Optimize has three parts that change your system settings: Internet optimization, registry cleaning, and system performance optimization.

The settings changed in the Internet optimization part of the application, such as those listed here, are set according to your connection type:

- Maximum Transfer Unit (MTU)
- Fast Retransmission and Recovery
- Number of Allowed Simultaneous HTTP Connections

Invalid keys that are removed by the registry cleaning part of the application are entries in the registry containing information about COM and ActiveX objects. These objects are parts of programs, and when you remove the programs these keys sometimes still exist. Optimize safely removes these keys if the COM object no longer exists. Areas of the registry where we look for the invalid keys are:

- Invalid Class IDs (CLSID)
- Invalid Program Identifiers (ProgID)
- Invalid Type Libraries (TypeLib)
- Invalid Interfaces

The performance section of the application changes some registry settings that help get the most out of your PC, such as:

- LargeSystemCache
- DisablePagingExecutive
- ContigFileAllocSize
- NtfsDisableLastAccessUpdate
- DisableScreenSaver
- AlwaysUnloadDll

Part 2

OPTIMIZING YOUR PC

In This Part

This part of the book shows step-by-step how to optimize your PC to ensure your computer operates at its full potential. We walk you through the installation of the included software, PC Pitstop Optimize. This software addresses the many issues of poor and degraded PC performance, such as those discussed in Part 1 of this book. This software will show how to clean up and speed up your computer. In addition, you'll learn many other tasks you can perform to ensure that you get the most out of your PC.

3

INSTALLING PC PITSTOP OPTIMIZE

Installing PC Pitstop Optimize is the first step toward quickly and easily resolving many common computing issues that your PC may be currently experiencing in order to improve the performance and stability of your computer.

System Requirements

The following requirements must be met, or exceeded, for the installation of PC Pitstop Optimize 1.5:

- 100 MHz processor or greater
- Microsoft Windows XP, 2000, ME, 98
- 64MB or greater of RAM
- 10MB or more of free disk space
- Super VGA Video, 15-inch monitor, 800x600 min. resolution

Installing PC Pitstop Optimize

To install PC Pitstop Optimize 1.5, which is included with this book, follow these steps.

Step 1

Insert the PC Pitstop Optimize installation CD into the drive on your PC. The installation will begin automatically.

If your installation fails to start automatically, you can launch it by browsing to the drive containing the CD and double-clicking the setup.exe file.

Step 2

You will now see the Welcome dialog box, as shown in Figure 3-1.

Figure 3-1: The Welcome dialog box

To continue, click Next.

Step 3

You will be prompted to accept the license agreement, as seen in Figure 3-2.

Figure 3-2: PC Pitstop Optimize license agreement

If you agree with the terms of the license agreement, click the I Accept the Agreement option, and click Next to continue.

If you disagree with the license terms, click the I Do Not Accept the Agreement option, click Next, and the installation will not continue.

Step 4

Now you will see the Select Destination Location dialog box, as shown in Figure 3-3.

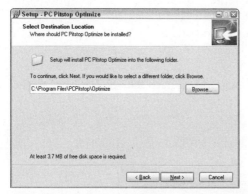

Figure 3-3: Select Destination Location dialog box

The default installation folder is C:\Program Files\PCPitstop\ Optimize, which should be fine. If so, click Next to continue.

If you wish to select a different folder, click the Browse button, find another location, and click OK. Then click Next when you're done.

Step 5

You will now see the Select Start Menu Folder dialog box, as seen in Figure 3-4.

Figure 3-4: Select Start Menu Folder dialog box

The default Start Menu Folder is PC Pitstop\Optimize, which should be fine. If so, click Next to continue.

If you wish to select a different folder, click the Browse button, browse to another location, and click OK. Then click Next when you're done.

You can also specify not to include the shortcuts in the Start menu by checking the Don't Create a Start Menu Folder option and clicking Next.

Step 6

You will now see the Select Additional Tasks dialog box, as shown in Figure 3-5.

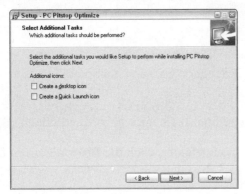

Figure 3-5: Select Additional Tasks dialog box

Specify whether or not you would like to create a desktop or Quick Launch icon, by checking the applicable boxes, and click Next to continue.

Step 7

Now you will be at the Ready to Install dialog box, as seen in Figure 3-6.

If the installation preferences are correct, click Install to start the installation. Otherwise, you can go back and change the preferences.

Figure 3-6: Ready to Install dialog box

You're Done!

After the installation of the files, you will see the setup complete dialog box, as seen Figure 3-7.

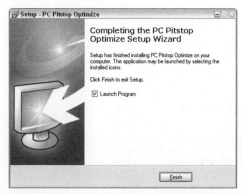

Figure 3-7: Setup complete dialog box

If you don't want to launch and use the software right away, uncheck the option.

To exit the setup wizard, click Finish.

Congratulations! PC Pitstop Optimize is now installed on your PC.

4

PERFORMING A SCAN

Before PC Pitstop Optimize can do any optimization, it first needs to scan your PC for junk files, invalid system and Internet settings, and other items that should be addressed to ensure maximum PC performance. Then you'll have the chance to specify exactly which items are removed or changed.

Here are the steps performed during a scan, which are discussed in this chapter:

Step 1: Open PC Pitstop Optimize

Step 2: Specify Initial Settings

Step 3: Start the Scan

Step 4: Perform the Scan

Step 5: Get Rid of Temporary Files

Step 6: Optimize Your Internet Settings

Step 7: Remove Unnecessary Startup Programs

Step 8: Optimize Your Registry Entries

Step 9: Optimize Your PC Performance

Keep in mind that the actual deletion of junk files and any needed system changes aren't removed or applied until you start the optimization process.

Step 1: Open PC Pitstop Optimize

Before you can begin, you have to open PC Pitstop Optimize. You can usually access this program from the Start menu by browsing to the following path:

Programs (or All Programs) → PC Pitstop → Optimize

Then click PC Pitstop Optimize, as shown in Figure 4-1.

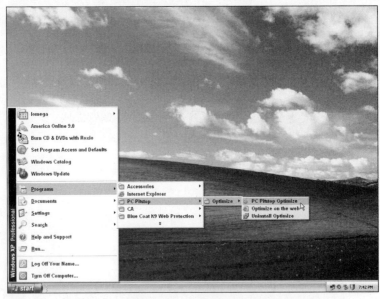

Figure 4-1: Opening PC Pitstop Optimize via the Start menu

Step 2: Specify Initial Settings

After starting PC Pitstop Optimize, you will see the welcome screen, as shown in Figure 4-2, and a few settings you need to specify.

First, you need to select an Internet Connection Type from the drop-down list, as shown in Figure 4-3:

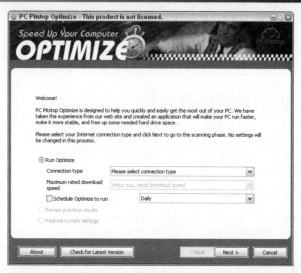

Figure 4-2: PC Pitstop Optimize Welcome screen

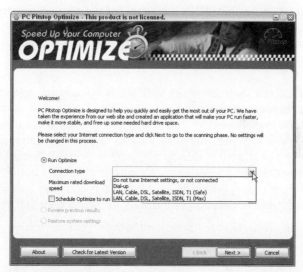

Figure 4-3: Selecting your Internet connection type

- **Do not tune Internet settings, or not connected**

  If you aren't currently connected to the Internet or for any other reason, you can select this option to prevent the optimization of your Internet connection settings.

- **Dial-up**

  If you are using a dial-up Internet connection such as with America Online (AOL) or NetZero, you should select this option.

- **LAN, Cable, DSL, Satellite, ISDN, T1 (Safe)**

  Select this option if you're using any other type of Internet connection than dial-up, such as the mentioned broadband or high-speed connections, and when PPPoE is being used or if you aren't sure.

- **LAN, Cable, DSL, Satellite, ISDN, T1 (Max)**

  Select this option if you're using any other type of Internet connection than dial-up, such as the mentioned broadband or high-speed connections, and when you are positive that PPPoE is not being used, because it may cause you to experience trouble connecting to some websites after the optimization.

  If you aren't sure that PPPoE is used for your Internet connection, you should use the Safe option instead (discussed in the preceding bullet) to prevent any potential problems.

Note

Point-to-Point Protocol over Ethernet (PPPoE) is a protocol specifying how a PC interacts with a broadband modem (i.e., xDSL, cable, wireless, etc). It provides the Internet service provider (ISP) with better control over how their customers log into the network and use network resources. From an Internet optimization standpoint, the important thing about PPPoE is that its maximum packet size is slightly smaller than non-PPPoE connections. In most cases, Windows can detect this situation and adjust automatically with the cooperation of the website being contracted.

The Safe settings are designed to accommodate situations where the website does not know how to request a PPPoE-friendly packet size.

If the Max option is selected, and connection problems materialize later, open and run the Optimize program again, but with the Safe option selected, to override and undo the Max settings.

Then you need to specify the Maximum rated download speed from the drop-down list, as seen in Figure 4-4.

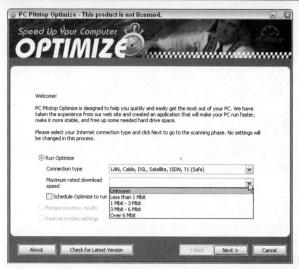

Figure 4-4: Selecting your Internet connection download speed

- **Unknown**

  If you're unsure of the maximum rated download speed of your particular Internet connection, you can select this option.

- **Less than 1 Mbit**

  Typically, the following Internet connection types fall into this range:

  - Dial-up
  - ISDN
  - Residential DSL (SDSL)
  - Satellite
  - Fractional T1

- **1 Mbit – 3 Mbit**

  Typically, the following Internet connection types fall into this range:

  - Cable
  - Full T1
  - ADSL

- **3 Mbit – 6 Mbit**

  The following Internet connection types may have the ability to achieve download rates in this range:

  - Cable
  - ADSL

- **Over 6 Mbit**

  The following Internet connection types may have the ability to achieve download rates in this range:

  - ADSL
  - T3

If you would like to automatically optimize your PC on a recurring basis, check Schedule Optimize to Run, and then choose your desired interval, as shown in Figure 4-5.

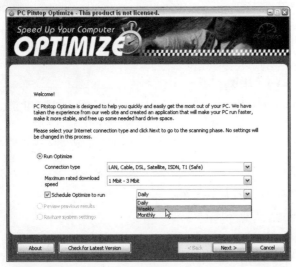

Figure 4-5: Selecting the interval for automatic optimizations

Click Next to continue.

Step 3: Start the Scan

Now you will see the Start Scanning screen, as shown in Figure 4-6.

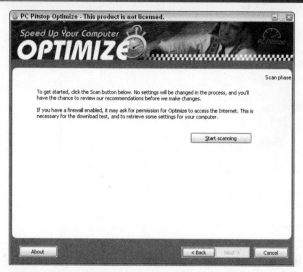

Figure 4-6: Start Scanning screen

As stated in the program, no changes will be made to your PC yet. It will simply scan your PC files and resources to figure out what should be optimized.

Click Start Scanning to continue.

Note

If the program doesn't detect an Internet connection or if it's blocked by a personal firewall, you'll be prompted to fix the Internet connection, as seen in Figure 4-7.

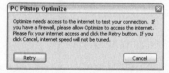

Figure 4-7: Fix Internet connection prompt

Step 4: Perform the Scan

Sit back and let PC Pitstop Optimize scan your PC for typical file and system issues.

You'll be notified after the scan is done by a message under the scanning status bar, as seen in Figure 4-8.

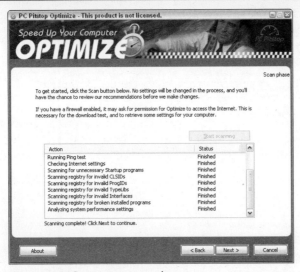

Figure 4-8: Scanning complete

Click Next to continue.

Step 5: Get Rid of Temporary Files

Now you will be at the Temporary Files screen, as shown in Figure 4-9.

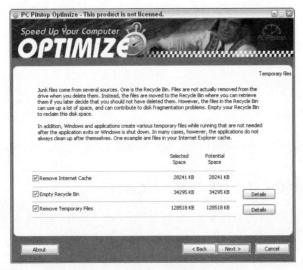

Figure 4-9: Temporary Files screen

You need to identify which junk files you would like Optimize to remove, by checking or un-checking the applicable checkboxes:

- **Remove Internet Cache**

  This deletes the temporary files created by Internet Explorer (IE) during web browsing.

  Remember, these are temporary files that aren't needed after you are finished web surfing. These files can take up large amounts of space and should be removed periodically.

  Although you can clear the cache in Internet Explorer, Optimize uses a more thorough method that deletes files left behind by IE.

Viewing Internet Explorer's Cache

If you are curious, you can view Internet Explorer's cache:

1. Open Internet Explorer.

2. Open Internet Options from the Tools menu, as seen in Figure 4-10.

Figure 4-10: Opening Internet Options

continued

continued

3. Click Settings... under the Temporary Internet Files section, as pointed out in Figure 4-11.

Figure 4-11: Accessing the temporary Internet files settings

4. Click View Files..., as seen in Figure 4-12.

The Temporary Internet Files window will appear.

Figure 4-12: Viewing temporary Internet files

- **Empty Recycle Bin**

    This will empty your Recycle Bin to reclaim the disk space occupied by files you have initially deleted from your computer.

    Remember, files are not actually removed from the drive when you delete them. Instead, the files are moved to the Recycle Bin where you can retrieve them if you later decide that you should not have deleted them.

- **Remove Temporary Files**

  This deletes the temporary files that the Windows operating system and other applications leave behind.

  Remember, these temporary files are not needed after the application exits or Windows is shut down. In many cases, however, the applications do not always clean up after themselves.

Viewing Your Recycle Bin

If you want to make sure you don't need these "deleted files" anymore, you can view the contents of your Recycle Bin:

1. Go to your desktop.

2. Double-click Recycle Bin, as shown in Figure 4-13.

Figure 4-13: Opening the Recycle Bin

3. The Recycle Bin will appear, as shown in Figure 4-14.

You can view the files and restore them if necessary.

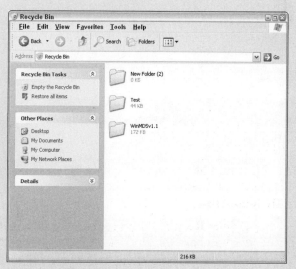

Figure 4-14: The Recycle Bin

Note

If you are curious, you can view your computer's temporary files by clicking the Details button.

Permanently deleting these types of files frees up disk space that typically results in better overall PC performance.

Click Next after identifying the junk files you would like to optimize and to continue to the next screen.

Step 6: Optimize Your Internet Settings

You will now be at the Internet Settings screen, as seen in Figure 4-15.

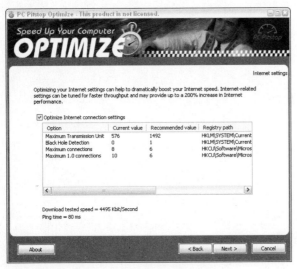

Figure 4-15: Internet Settings screen

Specify whether you would like to optimize your Internet connection settings by checking or un-checking the checkbox.

You can see a list of the all changes PC Pitstop Optimize has recommended that should help increase your Internet speeds.

Here are some of the entries you may receive:

- **Maximum Transfer Unit (MTU)**

  The maximum packet size that is sent and received over the Internet.

- **TCP Receiving Window Size**

  The amount of data that is received before confirmation.

- **Default Time to Live**

  The length of time the data is kept before being discarded.

- **Automatic MTU Detection**

  Allows your system to identify the MTU size.

- **Blackhole Detection**

  Checks if connected systems supports Automatic MTU discovery.

- **Large TCP Windows**

  Support for larger amounts of data before confirmation of received.

- **Fast retransmission and recovery**

  Allows for a fast transaction recovery after lost packets.

- **Selective Acknowledgements**

  Allows for recovery without re-sending existing data after lost packets.

- **Number of Allowed Simultaneous HTTP Connections**

  Number of open connections to a single website at one time.

Click Next to continue.

Step 7: Remove Unnecessary Startup Programs

Now you will be at the Unnecessary Startup Programs screen, as shown in Figure 4-16.

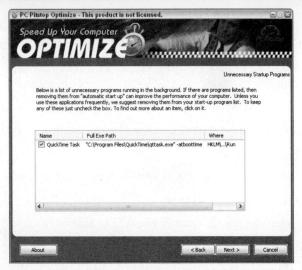

Figure 4-16: Unnecessary Startup Programs screen

Select the programs that you would like to disable from starting up each time you start your PC.

Here are some of the most common unnecessary programs that you may want to disable:

- **qttask.exe - QuickTime Icon**

  This is Apple's Quick Time Tray Icon, as shown in Figure 4-17, which lets you start Quick Time from the System Tray.

  This unnecessary program uses as much as 750KB of memory.

  Even if disabled, you can still start Quick Time from its Start menu icon or by clicking an associated file such as .MOV.

- **realsched.exe - RealPlayer**

  This is a scheduler for some generally unneeded functions, such as occasionally checking to make sure that RealPlayer "owns" certain media types.

Figure 4-17: Apple's Quick Time system tray icon

- **realplay.exe - RealPlayer**

  This is RealPlayer's system tray icon (called StartCenter), which runs when Windows starts to preload some RealPlayer components and provides a tray icon to access RealPlayer.

  However, this application also uses up valuable system resources.

  Even if disabled, you can still start RealPlayer from its Start menu icon or by clicking an associated file such as .MP3.

- **hkcmd.exe - Intel Hotkeys**

  This is part of the drivers for boards with Intel 81x graphics chips, and allows you to define hotkey combinations to change video resolutions.

  This is not something that most users do often, and it can be done through Control Panel (Intel Graphics icon) or Desktop Properties pretty quickly.

  It's recommend to stop this task to save resources and prevent accidental use of the hotkey feature.

- **soundman.exe - Realtek Sound Manager**

  This application lets you manage and control some of the esoteric features of the Realtek sound chip.

  Most users don't need to change any of these features and can safely disable this program. You can always use the standard Windows volume control to change the sound volume.

- **waol.exe - America Online**

  This is the main AOL executable; however, it does not need to start during Windows boot.

  You can always start America Online as needed, via its Start menu entry or desktop icon.

For more information on these applications or others, you can click each item to learn more about the program, which can help you determine which programs to remove.

Click Next to continue.

Step 8: Optimize Your Registry Entries

You should now be at the Registry Entries screen, as seen in Figure 4-18.

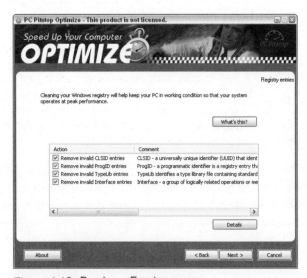

Figure 4-18: Registry Entries screen

Specify which type of registry entries you would like Optimize to clean.

Note

The registry contains information that Windows continually references during operation, such as profiles for each user, the applications installed on the computer and the types of documents that each can create, property sheet settings for folders and application icons, what hardware exists on the system, and the ports that are being used.

Optimize looks for specific registry keys that can slow the computer's performance. These are typically invalid keys containing information about COM and ActiveX objects. These objects are parts of programs, and when you remove the programs, these keys sometimes still exist. Optimize safely removes these keys if the COM object no longer exists.

Areas of the registry where Optimize looks for the invalid keys are:

- **Invalid Class IDs (CLSID)**

    This is a universally unique identifier (UUID) that identifies a COM component. Each COM component has its CLSID in the Windows registry so that it can be loaded by other applications.

- **Invalid Program Identifiers (ProgID)**

    A programmatic identifier is a registry entry that identifies a COM component and can be associated with a CLSID.

- **Invalid Type Libraries (TypeLib)**

    This identifies a type library file contain standard descriptions of data types, modules, and interfaces that can be used to fully expose objects with ActiveX technology.

- **Invalid Interfaces**

    This is a group of logically related operations or methods that provides access to a component object.

In addition, to help in your determination, you can view the particular entries for each registry type that Optimize is suggesting to clean, by clicking the Details button.

Click Next to continue.

Step 9: Optimize Your PC Performance

Now you will see the Performance screen (see Figure 4-19).

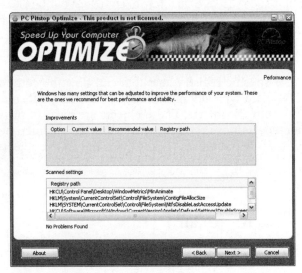

Figure 4-19: Performance screen

Choose which recommended items you would like to optimize.

Here are some of the entries you may receive and explanations for each:

- **DisablePaging**

  This specifies whether user-mode and kernel-mode drivers and kernel-mode system code can be paged to disk when not in use. The computer will perform faster when the hard disk is not used for RAM. This loads the OS into the much faster RAM.

- **ContigFileAllocSize**

  This is the size of the contiguous space that is used when allocating disk space. The less space that needs to be searched for information, the less time the operation will take, and the faster the computer will function.

- **NtfsDisableLastAccessUpdate**

  This entry determines whether New Technology File System (NTFS) updates the last-access timestamp on each directory when it lists the directories on an NTFS volume.

  This optimization speeds up file processing. The information is still available, but it is just not done as the default.

- **DisableScreenSaver**

  This turns the system screen saver on or off. This is done during the defragmenting process to speed things up. Each time the screen saver comes on the process has to shut down the screen saver and start over.

- **AlwaysUnloadDll**

  This determines whether Windows caches system DLLs. This frees up memory in older systems and can speed up the shutdown process, as well.

- **LargeSystemCache**

  This determines whether the system maintains a standard size or a large size file system cache, and influences how often the system writes changed pages to disk. The less disk writing there is, the faster the performance.

Click Next to continue, then move on to the next chapter, which steps you through the process of the actual optimization.

5

THE OPTIMIZATION

After completing the PC Pitstop Optimize scan and configuration, as discussed in Chapter 4, you will now be at the Register Now! screen, as Figure 5-1 shows.

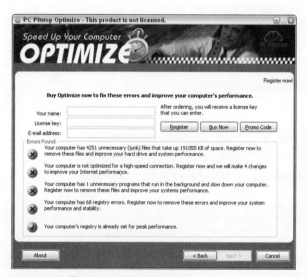

Figure 5-1: Register Now! screen

Step 1: Enter License Information

Enter your name, license key, and email address in the appropriate fields, such as shown in Figure 5-2, and click Register.

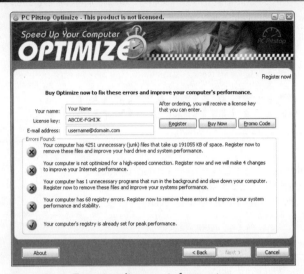

Figure 5-2: Entering license information

After successful registration, you'll be notified via a message on the screen, such as shown in Figure 5-3.

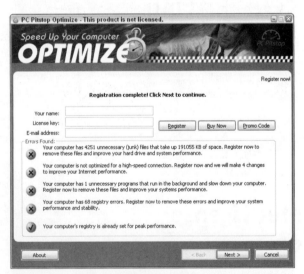

Figure 5-3: Registration successful message

In addition, a Thank You page such as Figure 5-4 shows will appear from pcpitstop.com.

Figure 5-4: Thank You page

To continue, click Next.

Step 2: Start the Optimization

You will now be at the Optimize Phase screen, as shown in Figure 5-5.

Figure 5-5: Optimize Phase screen

Click Optimize Now! to begin making the recommended changes.

Sit back and let PC Pitstop Optimize go to work!

Step 3: Optimization Completed

You'll be notified after the scan is done by a message under the scanning status bar, such as seen in Figure 5-6.

Figure 5-6: Optimize phase completed

Click Next to review the results.

Step 4: The Results

The results page will appear as shown in Figure 5-7.

You can review the items that the program optimized.

When you're done, click Finish to exit the program.

Figure 5-7: Optimization results

If prompted to restart your computer (see Figure 5-8 for an example) you can either click Reboot Now to do so immediately, or click Close to restart later.

Figure 5-8: Reboot prompt

6

OTHER WAYS TO OPTIMIZE YOUR PC

This chapter shows how to perform many tasks that will help optimize your PC. Performing these additional tasks, along with using PC Pitstop Optimize, regularly or at least once a month will ensure your PC runs faster and more efficiently.

Keep Windows Up to Date

Keeping Windows up-to-date ensures your PC is protected from the latest known security holes and fixes bugs or errors of the operating system, which will help increase PC performance.

You can easily check for and perform needed updates for Windows by visiting the following website:

`http://windowsupdate.microsoft.com`

You can also configure Windows XP to automatically download updates when they become available:

1. Open the Control Panel, as seen in Figure 6-1.

   If the Start menu is in classic look, the Control Panel is under Settings on the menu.

Figure 6-1: Opening the Control Panel

2. Click Security Center, as Figure 6-2 shows, if the Control Panel is in category view; otherwise ignore this step and move to the next step.

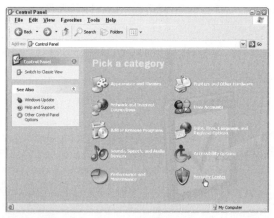

Figure 6-2: Opening the Security Center category

3. Click Automatic Updates, as shown in Figure 6-3.

Figure 6-3: Opening Automatic Updates

4. It's recommended to use the Automatic option, as Figure 6-4 points out.

Figure 6-4: Automatic Update option

Adjust Visual Settings

You can increase the performance of your computer by sacrificing some visual effects in Windows XP. These effects include items such as shadowing, smoothing, and fading of fonts, menus, and your cursor.

Here is how to change these visual effect settings:

1. Right-click My Computer and click Properties, as seen in Figure 6-5.

Figure 6-5: Accessing My Computer properties

2. Click the Advanced tab, as Figure 6-6 shows.

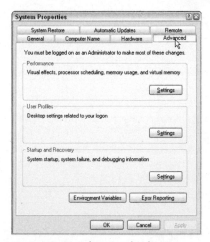

Figure 6-6: Advanced tab

3. Click Settings, under the Performance area, as shown in Figure 6-7.

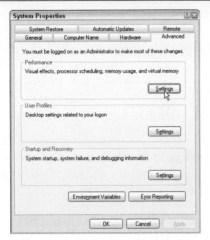

Figure 6-7: Accessing Performance settings

4. On the Visual Effects tab, select the Adjust for Best Performance option, as seen in Figure 6-8.

Figure 6-8: Selecting the Best Performance option

5. When you're done, click OK.

Remove Unused Programs

Freeing up disk space helps increase overall performance of your
PC. Therefore, you should remove any programs or software that
you don't use.

Note
Before removing software from your PC you may want to ensure you
have saved any keys or serial numbers that are needed for the software.
Therefore, it will be much easier if you want to reinstall the software at
a later date.

Follow these steps to remove (and to view) installed applications on
your PC, in Windows XP:

1. Open the Control Panel, as seen in Figure 6-9.

Figure 6-9: Opening the Control Panel

If the Start menu is in classic look, the Control Panel is
under Settings on the menu.

2. Click Add or Remove Programs, as Figure 6-10 shows.

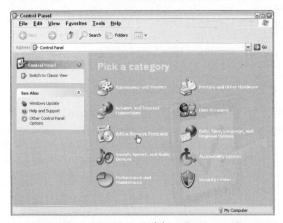

Figure 6-10: Accessing Add or Remove Programs

3. The Add or Remove Programs window will appear. You may need to wait a few moments for the programs to load. See Figure 6-11 for an example.

Figure 6-11: Add or Remove Programs utility

4. You can scroll up and down to view your installed programs.

To remove a program, click the particular item and click the Change/Remove or Remove button, such Figure 6-12 illustrates.

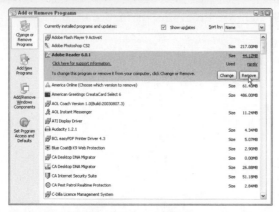

Figure 6-12: Removing a program

Then the uninstall program for the particular software should appear and may confirm your action, as Figure 6-13 shows.

Figure 6-13: Example of uninstall confirmation

Clean Up Your Personal Files

Organizing personal files and documents that are scattered throughout your PC and deleting old or unused files will help free up disk space. This also helps increase the overall performance of your PC.

Here are some tips to keeping your personal files in order:

- **Create separate personal folders**

  Start with creating folders for each user of your PC. For example, if it's a family PC you may want to create a separate folder for each member, such as Figure 6-14 shows, in a convenient place such as the desktop or My Documents.

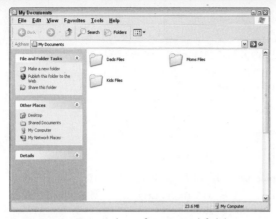

Figure 6-14: Examples of personal folders

This way everyone has a place to save and create their documents, which helps keep the files on your computer organized.

- **Create sub-folders**

  For each of your topics or interests create a folder, such as the following and as shown in Figure 6-15.

Figure 6-15: Examples of sub-folders

- Work Files
- School Files
- Church Files
- Vacations
- Family Pictures
- Downloads

- **Periodically clean up your files**

   Once in awhile you should go through your folders and delete any files you don't need anymore. Especially look for and remove large files.

- **Empty the Recycle Bin**

   Typically after deleting files they go to the Recycle Bin rather than being completely destroyed. After deleting files, especially larger files, you should empty the Recycle Bin.

   The Recycle Bin icon, as shown in Figure 6-16, is usually located on the desktop.

Figure 6-16: The Recycle Bin icon

   To open it, simply double-click the icon. Then to empty the Recycle Bin, you can click Empty the Recycle Bin on the left task pane, as shown in Figure 6-17, or under the File menu on the top.

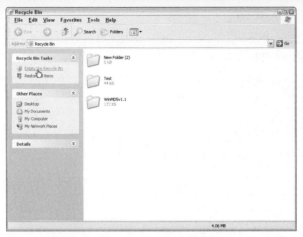

Figure 6-17: Emptying the Recycle Bin

Check for Hard Drive Errors

Data in hard drives can become corrupt, such as from power surges and improper shutdowns, which can cause disk errors. Typically, these are errors that won't be noticeable to the PC user; therefore you should perform a hard drive scan at least once a month.

Here is how to check your hard drive for errors (and fix it) using Windows XP:

1. Open My Computer.

2. Right-click the disk you would like to check (for instance, the C drive) and click Properties. Figure 6-18 shows an example.

Figure 6-18: Accessing drive properties

3. Click the Tools tab.

4. Click Check Now..., as seen in Figure 6-19, under the Error-checking section.

Figure 6-19: Accessing the Check Disk utility

5. It's recommended to mark both check disk options, Automatically Fix File System Errors and Scan for and Attempt Recovery of Bad Sectors, to ensure any disk errors are properly addressed. See Figure 6-20 for an example.

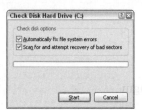

Figure 6-20: Marking the Check Disk options

6. Click Start.

If the hard drive is currently in use, which will likely be the case, a pop-up message will appear, such as Figure 6-21 shows.

Click Yes to schedule the scan for the next restart, or to cancel the scan, click No.

Figure 6-21: Pop-up message

Defragment the Hard Drive

Defragmenting your hard drive optimizes it by reorganizing files that are scattered around the disk drive. Moving this information into contiguous clusters allows for faster retrieval of files and results in an increase of overall system performance.

Fragmentation worsens the more you install, uninstall, move, and delete files on your hard drive. However, hard drive fragmentation is common and occurs naturally.

The amount of time that defragmentation takes depends on several factors, including the following:

- Amount of fragmentation
- Size of the hard drive
- Number and size of files on the hard drive
- Performance of your PC

You can get an idea of the amount of fragmented files and folders before performing a defragmentation by analyzing the hard drive first. This allows you to better decide whether you would benefit from defragmenting the hard drive.

Note

In order to analyze or defragment your hard drive your PC has to be logged on a Windows account with administrative privileges.

If you are not sure whether you are, you can check:

1. Open the Control Panel, as seen in Figure 6-22.

continued

continued

Figure 6-22: Opening the Control Panel

If the Start menu is in classic look, the Control Panel is under Settings on the menu.

2. Open User Accounts, as Figure 6-23 shows when in category view.

Figure 6-23: Opening the User Accounts utility

3. Look for your user account and see if it belongs to the administrators group, such as identified in Figure 6-24.

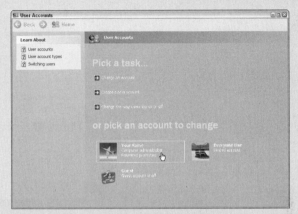

Figure 6-24: Checking for administrative privileges

Before performing the defragmentation you should first analyze the hard drive to get a feeling of the amount of fragmented files and folders on your hard drive.

Here is how to analyze your hard drive using Windows XP:

1. Open Disk Defragmenter, which can be accessed by browsing to the following path on your Start menu:

- Start
- Programs (or All Programs)
- Accessories
- System Tools

Then click Disk Defragmenter, as shown in Figure 6-25.

2. Click Analyze, as shown in Figure 6-26.

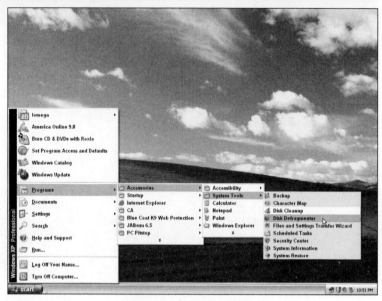

Figure 6-25: Accessing Disk Defragmenter

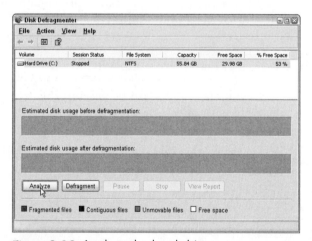

Figure 6-26: Analyze the hard drive

3. During the analysis you should see a depiction of the hard drive's estimated fragmentation status, such as Figure 6-27 shows.

Figure 6-27: Estimated fragmentation status

You can refer to the color codes on the program and the following descriptions of the codes to better understand the status:

- **Red**

  This means most of the clusters are part of a fragmented file.

- **Blue**

  This means most of the clusters are contiguous files with clusters in the group that contain only free space and contiguous clusters.

- **Green**

  This means most of the clusters are part of a file that cannot be moved from its current location.

- **White**

  This means most of the clusters are free space and contiguous clusters.

4. At the end of the analysis, a pop-up message will appear, as Figure 6-28 shows. This lets you know it has completed and if you should continue with the defragmentation. Figure 6-28 shows an example of when a defragmentation is not recommended.

Figure 6-28: Example of a pop-up status message

From this point you can do one of the following:

- **View a report for more details about your current fragmentation status**

  You can simply click the View Report button, as shown in Figure 6-29.

Figure 6-29: Accessing the fragmentation report

You will then see the Analysis Report window, such as shown in Figure 6-30, which shows detailed information about the hard drive (or volume) that was scanned.

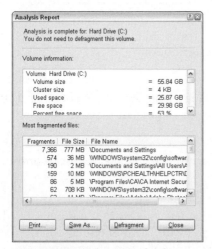

Figure 6-30: Example of a fragmentation report

You can get a good indicator of the hard drive (or volume) fragmentation state by referring to your average number of fragments per file. As Figure 6-31 shows, this piece of information is located in the Volume Information list.

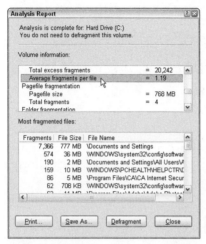

Figure 6-31: Example of average number of fragments per file

You can then compare your number to the following average number of fragments per file ranges, which gives you an idea of how bad your fragmentation is at the time:

- **1.00**

  Most or all files are contiguous.

- **1.10**

  About 10% of the files are in fragments of two or more pieces.

- **1.20**

  About 20% of the files are in fragments of two or more pieces.

- **1.30**

  About 30% of the files are in fragments of two or more pieces.

- **2.00**

  Most or all of the files are in fragments of two or more pieces.

- **Continue with the defragmentation**

  Simply click the Defragment button, as Figure 6-32 shows, to begin the defragmentation, and then continue with Step 3 on the next set of steps.

Figure 6-32: Starting the defragmentation

- **Close the window**

  To close the pop-up window, for example if it recommends not performing a defragmentation, you can click Close, as seen in Figure 6-33.

Figure 6-33: Closing the pop-up status message

Here is how to defragment your hard drive using Windows XP:

1. Open Disk Defragmenter, which can be accessed by browsing to the following path on your Start menu:

   - Start
   - Programs (or All Programs)
   - Accessories
   - System Tools

   Then click Disk Defragmenter, as shown in Figure 6-34.

2. Click Defragment, as shown in Figure 6-35.

   The amount of time that defragmentation takes, which can take up to several hours, depends on several factors including the following:

   - Amount of fragmentation
   - Size of the hard drive

- Number and size of files on the hard drive
- Performance of your PC

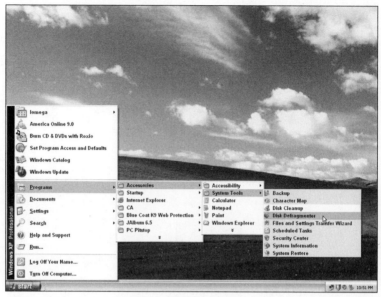

Figure 6-34: Accessing Disk Defragmenter

Figure 6-35: Starting the defragmentation

3. First a quick analysis is performed before the defragmentation begins. During the process, you should see a depiction of the hard drive's before and after estimated fragmentation status, such as Figure 6-36 shows.

Figure 6-36: Before and after estimated fragmentation status

You can refer to the color codes on the program and the following descriptions of the codes to better understand the statuses:

- **Red**

  This means most of the clusters are part of a fragmented file.

- **Blue**

  This means most of the clusters are contiguous files with clusters in the group that contain only free space and contiguous clusters.

- **Green**

  This means most of the clusters are part of a file that cannot be moved from its current location.

- **White**

  This means most of the clusters are free space and contiguous clusters.

4. At the end of the defragmentation, a pop-up message should appear that will let you know it has completed and displays the results.

Remove Additional Start-up Programs

Many software programs may add themselves (with or without your knowledge) to your Startup folder, which may cause a longer boot time when entering Windows and bog down your PC.

Here is how you can view and modify your start-up programs:

1. Open My Computer.

2. Browse to and open the Documents and Settings folder (see Figure 6-37 for an example) on the root of your hard drive.

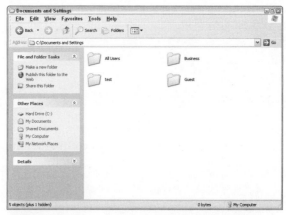

Figure 6-37: Documents and Settings folder

3. Open the folder of your desired user account.

4. Open the Start Menu folder, such as seen in Figure 6-38.

Figure 6-38: Opening the Start Menu folder

5. Go to the Programs folder, and then open the Startup folder.

6. You should remove any programs that you don't care to automatically run at Windows start-up.

To do this, simply click a particular program shortcut icon and press your Delete key, or right-click the item and click Delete.

Now you should repeat Steps 3 through 6 in the preceding list, making sure you select the All Users folder, so you can access the Startup folder for all the user accounts on the PC.

7

UPDATING PC PITSTOP OPTIMIZE

To ensure you get the most out of PC Pitstop Optimize you should keep the software up to date with any fixes or new features, which may include updates to the files and system settings it uses to optimize your PC. Therefore, before each use you should check for updates.

Updating the Software

You can access the update utility within the PC Pitstop Optimize software by following these steps:

1. Browse to the following path on your Start menu:

   Programs (or All Programs) → PC Pitstop → Optimize

   Then click PC Pitstop Optimize, as shown in Figure 7-1.

2. After starting PC Pitstop Optimize, you will see the Welcome screen, as shown in Figure 7-2.

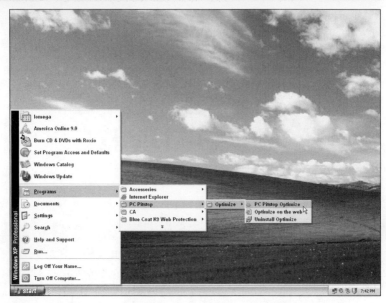

Figure 7-1: Opening PC Pitstop Optimize via the Start menu

Figure 7-2: PC Pitstop Optimize Welcome screen

3. Click Check for Latest Version, as seen in Figure 7-3.

Figure 7-3: Clicking Check for Latest Version

If no updates are currently available you'll be prompted such as Figure 7-4 shows.

Figure 7-4: Up-to-date prompt

8

TROUBLESHOOTING PC PITSTOP OPTIMIZE

This chapter discusses common problems and fixes you may experience when using PC Pitstop Optimize and also lets you know where you can get more help.

Program Doesn't Load Correctly

Problem:

PC Pitstop Optimize won't load correctly or freezes, such as loading the program window but no text or images and stops responding.

Fixes:

You should try a complete removal of the PC Pitstop Optimize software, and then install it again.

First you need to do a regular uninstall:

1. Run the uninstall program for PC Pitstop Optimize, which can be accessed by browsing to the following path on your Start menu:

   Programs (or All Programs) → PC Pitstop → Optimize

   Then click Uninstall Optimize, as shown in Figure 8-1.

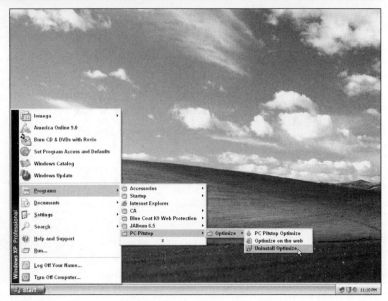

Figure 8-1: Running Uninstall Optimize

2. You will be prompted with a confirmation, as Figure 8-2 shows.

Figure 8-2: Uninstall confirmation

Click Yes to begin removing PC Pitstop Optimize.

3. After the removal has been completed you'll be notified by a prompt, as seen in Figure 8-3.

Figure 8-3: Removal completed prompt

Now follow these steps to delete the PCPitstop folder:

1. Open My Computer on your desktop.

2. Go to the PCPitstop folder, such as seen in Figure 8-4, by following this path:

```
C:\Program Files\PC Pitstop
```

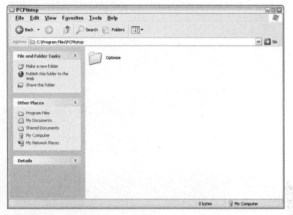

Figure 8-4: PCPitstop folder

3. Delete the entire Optimize folder. See Figure 8-5 for an example.

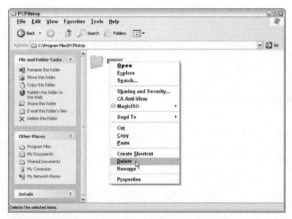

Figure 8-5: Deleting the Optimize folder

Then complete the full removal of PC Pitstop Optimize by removing the registry entry:

1. Click the Start menu and click Run, such as Figure 8-6 shows.

Figure 8-6: Accessing the Run utility

2. Type **regedit**, such as shown in Figure 8-7, and click OK.

Figure 8-7: Entering regedit

3. Once the Registry Editor opens, navigate to the following:

`HKEY_LOCAL_MACHINE\SOFTWARE\PCPitstop`

Figure 8-8 shows an example.

4. Delete the Optimize folder, such as shown in Figure 8-9.

Now that you've completely removed the software, you need to reinstall it. You can refer Chapter 3 for installation instructions.

Figure 8-8: PCPitstop registry folder

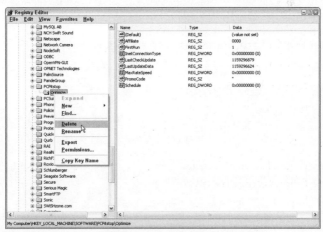

Figure 8-9: Deleting PCPitstop registry folder

Can't Communicate with the Internet

Problem:

You are able to access the Internet from a web browser; however, PC Pitstop isn't able to access the Internet. Figure 8-10 shows an example of a prompt you may receive.

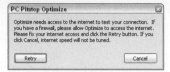

Figure 8-10: Internet not working prompt

Fixes:

If you have active firewall protection on your PC, it's likely the problem. If your firewall software alerts you to an Internet access attempt from Optimize, make sure you authorize the access.

In addition, the Windows XP firewall utility may be preventing access; therefore you should ensure Optimize is given authorization to access the Internet.

You'll need to set your firewall to allow www.pcpitstop.com. The corresponding IP is 64.29.201.21.

1. Open the Control Panel, as seen in Figure 8-11.

Figure 8-11: Opening the Control Panel

If the Start menu is in classic look, the Control Panel is under Settings on the menu.

2. Click Security Center, as Figure 8-12 shows, if the Control Panel is in category view; otherwise ignore this step and move to the next step.

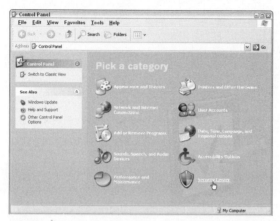

Figure 8-12: Opening Security Center category

3. Click Windows Firewall, as shown in Figure 8-13.

Figure 8-13: Opening Windows Firewall

4. On the General tab, uncheck the Don't Allow Exceptions option, such as pointed out in Figure 8-14.

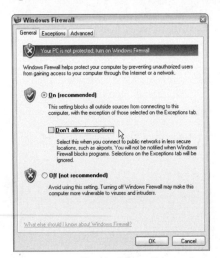

Figure 8-14: Don't Allow Exceptions option

5. Click the Exceptions tab, as Figure 8-15 shows.

Figure 8-15: Exceptions tab

6. Click Add Program..., as seen in Figure 8-16.

Figure 8-16: Clicking Add Program

7. Click Browse..., as Figure 8-17 shows.

Figure 8-17: Clicking Browse

8. Browse to the following path:

```
C:\Program Files\PC Pitstop\Optimize
```

Then select PCPOptimize.exe and click Open, as seen in Figure 8-18.

Figure 8-18: Selecting Optimize

9. Click OK to return to the main Windows Firewall utility.

10. Click the Advanced tab, as Figure 8-19 shows.

Figure 8-19: Advanced tab

11. Under the Network Connection Settings section, click Settings..., as seen in Figure 8-20.

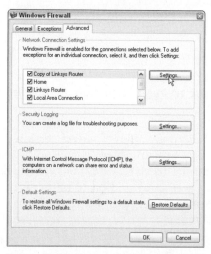

Figure 8-20: Accessing Network Connection Settings

12. Click the ICMP tab, as shown in Figure 8-21.

Figure 8-21: ICMP tab

13. Ensure the Allow Incoming Echo Request option is checked, if it exists.

14. When you are done, click OK.

Error During Installation

Problem:

During the installation of PC Pitstop Optimize a code 5 error appears.

Fixes:

This error appears when you are trying to install an application that is already open.

Make sure to close Optimize before installing a newer version or during reinstallation. In most cases this problem is caused by purchasing Optimize just after running the free scan, because all that is required to run the application is to copy and paste in the license key. However, another installation of Optimize isn't necessary.

Customer Support Information

For any other problems or specific questions, you can contact PC Pitstop Customer Support by visiting its website:

http://www.pcpitstop.com/store/service.asp

Online support for PC Pitstop Optimize is also offered on its Optimize discussion forum at:

http://optimize.pcpitstop.com/

Part 3

BONUS MATERIAL

In This Part

Like many other computer users, you've likely used PC Pitstop Optimize and the other techniques discussed in this book to increase the performance of an old or aged PC. Because you're likely dealing with an older PC, we felt that it would be very beneficial for you to have some additional tips that apply to your particular situation.

Included in this part of the book are bonus chapters about using and upgrading an older PC. This additional bonus material will help you make your older PC work the best it can. In addition, you receive tips on buying a new PC if you can't squeeze enough performance out of your older PC in order to support some of the newer software applications. These bonus chapters save you lots of money by avoiding the need to purchase separate books on these topics. We just want to be sure that you get the best out of your PC!

9

SOLVE COMMON PROBLEMS WITH WINDOWS

Although Windows XP is arguably the most stable and reliable version of Windows thus far, occasionally you might hit a few digital potholes that throw XP out of alignment. To ensure a smooth ride and eliminate common XP problems, follow the tips in this chapter in addition to using CA's PC Pitstop Optimize software.

Close an Unresponsive Program

Occasionally, a program gets caught up and won't close. When that happens, you can force it to shut down by using the Task Manager, as follows:

1. Simultaneously press the Ctrl, Alt, and Delete keys on your keyboard, which opens the Windows Task Manager. (However, if your version of Windows is configured differently, pressing these keys might open a Windows Security box. In that case, simply click the Task Manager button.)

2. Click the Applications tab.

3. Click the name of the unresponsive program.

4. At the bottom of the Task Manager, click the End Task button.

5. If the troubled program doesn't close immediately, a message alerts you that the program is not responding. Click the End Now button.

6. If the program still does not respond, or if Windows feels sluggish, shut down your computer and restart it.

Delete an Undeletable File

Sometimes files can become corrupt, in which case Windows XP prevents you from deleting them and displays an error message that says the files cannot be deleted because they are currently in use. Even if you restart your computer and try to delete the files again, usually you see the same error message. To force Windows to delete the files, try the following steps.

Warning
Be careful when editing the registry. Deleting or editing the wrong entries could cause more problems.

To delete common files:

1. Close all open documents and programs that are currently running.

2. Shut down your computer, and then reboot it.

3. Return to Windows and try to delete the file again.

4. If you still can't get rid of the file, shut down your computer.

5. Turn on your computer and immediately press the F8 key on your keyboard several times until the Windows Advanced Options Menu screen appears.

6. Use the up or down arrows on your keyboard to select Safe Mode, and then press the Enter key.

7. The next screen displays the message "Please select the operating system to start." Assuming you have only Windows XP installed on your system, press the Enter key. If you have more than one operating system installed, use the up or down arrows on your keyboard to select Windows XP, and then press the Enter key.

8. Windows loads some software, which could take a minute or two. Depending on how your version of Windows is configured, a login screen or the Welcome screen appears. If you see the login screen, type your account name and password (if you have one), and then press Enter. If you see the Welcome screen, click the icon for the account labeled Administrator or an account that has administrative privileges, and then type your password (if you have one).

9. A message alerts you that Windows is running in Safe Mode. To proceed, click the Yes button.

10. You can use Safe Mode in much the same way that you use the regular Windows mode. Locate the undeletable file, and then try deleting it again.

11. If you are successful, reboot your computer and return to the regular Windows mode. If your efforts are not successful, seek the help of a computer professional.

To delete videos with the file extension .avi:

1. Click the Start button in the lower-left corner of Windows.

2. Click the Run button.

3. A window opens. Type **regedit** in the blank and click the OK button or press the Enter key.

4. Click the OK button or press the Enter key.

5. The Windows Registry Editor opens. In the left window pane, double-click the registry key labeled HKEY_LOCAL_MACHINE. If you can't find it, do the following:

   a. In the left window pane of the Registry Editor, scroll to the top.

   b. If any of the HKEY registry keys are open — as indicated by a minus sign (-) on their left side — close them by clicking that minus sign. When a registry key has been properly closed, it will have a plus sign (+) next to it.

   c. Repeat this process for the remaining HKEY registry keys until the only things visible in the left window pane are the five HKEY keys (see Figure 9-1).

   d. Double-click the HKEY_LOCAL_MACHINE registry key.

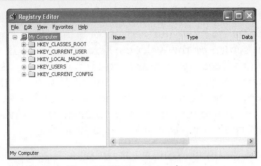

Figure 9-1: Five HKEY registry keys

6. A new column of registry keys appears. Double-click the Software registry key.

7. Open the Classes registry key.

8. A long list of registry keys appears. Scroll down and double-click CLSID (see Figure 9-2).

Figure 9-2: Finding the CLSID registry key

9. Another long list of registry keys appears. Scroll down and double-click the one labeled {87D62D94-71B3-4b9a-9489-5FE6850DC73E}.

10. Right-click the InProcServer32 registry key and select Delete (see Figure 9-3).

11. You are asked to confirm the deletion. Click the Yes button.

12. Exit the Registry Editor by clicking the X button in the upper-right corner.

13. Shut down your computer and restart it.

14. When you return to Windows, you should now be able to delete the .avi file.

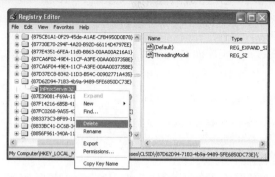

Figure 9-3: Deleting the InProcServer32 registry key

Restore Windows to a Healthy State

In a pinch, the Windows XP System Restore feature is a reliable way to recover from a software crisis. In a sense, System Restore sends your computer back in time to a day when it was working properly. If Windows seems like it is undergoing a complete meltdown, try restoring it back to a healthy state, as follows:

1. Click the Start button in the lower-left corner of Windows.

2. Click All Programs.

3. Select Accessories.

4. Select System Tools.

5. Click System Restore.

6. The System Restore window opens. Click the Restore My Computer to an Earlier Time button (see Figure 9-4).

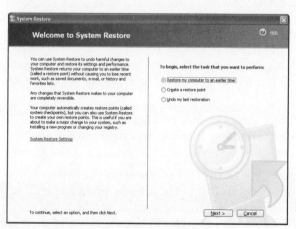

Figure 9-4: System Restore window

7. Click the Next button, located near the lower-right corner of this window.

8. A calendar appears. In it, click a day when your computer was working properly, and then click the Next button.

9. To confirm your choice, click Next.

10. The System Restore process begins. Moments later, your computer automatically restarts itself. When it boots up, follow the on-screen instructions.

11. To make it easier to access System Restore the next time you need it, you can "pin" it to your Start menu (but only if your Start menu is in XP mode rather than classic mode), like this:

    a. Follow steps 1 through 4 in this procedure to access the System Tools folder.

    b. This time, right-click System Restore and select Pin to Start Menu.

    c. A shortcut to System Restore is placed on your Start menu. From now on, whenever you need to restore your computer to an earlier time, simply click the Start button and click System Restore.

Use System Restore When Windows Won't Start

When your computer is going haywire, System Restore can be a virtual lifesaver. But what if your high-tech troubles are so severe that Windows can't even start up? In that case, try using the Safe Mode with Command Prompt to access System Restore:

1. After turning on your computer, press the F8 key several times until the Windows Advanced Options Menu screen appears.

2. Use the up or down arrows on your keyboard to select Safe Mode with Command Prompt, and then press Enter.

3. The next screen displays the message, "Please select the operating system to start." Assuming you only have Windows XP installed on your system, press Enter. If you have more than one operating system installed, use the up and down arrow keys to select Windows XP, and then press the Enter key.

4. Windows loads some software, which could take a minute or two. Depending on how your version of Windows is configured, a login screen or the Welcome screen appears. If you see the login screen, type your account name and password (if you have one), and press Enter. If you see the Welcome screen, click the icon for the account labeled Administrator or an account that has administrative privileges, and then type your password (if you have one).

5. Next, a command prompt appears. Type **%systemroot%\ system32\restore\rstrui.exe** in the blank and press the Enter key.

6. After several seconds, the System Restore window appears. Click the Restore My Computer to an Earlier Time button.

7. Click the Next button, located near the lower-right corner of this window.

8. A calendar appears. In it, click a day when your computer was working properly, and then click the Next button.

9. To confirm your choice, click Next.

10. The System Restore process begins. Moments later, your computer automatically restarts itself. When it boots up, follow the on-screen instructions.

Protect Windows from a Botched Software Installation

Before you install any new program, you should create a "restore point." Doing so will enable you to undo any problems or damage caused by the software installation. Here's how:

1. Click the Start button in the lower-left corner of Windows.

2. Click All Programs.

3. Select Accessories.

4. Select System Tools.

5. Click System Restore.

6. The System Restore window opens. Click the Create a Restore Point button (see Figure 9-5).

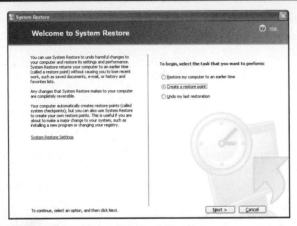

Figure 9-5: System Restore window

7. Click Next.

8. Under the Restore Point Description heading, type some words or sentences that will help you to remember why you are creating this restore point. For example, if you just bought a new anti-virus program, you could label this restore point "Before Installation of New Antivirus Software."

9. Click the Create button.

If a Program Won't Start or Run Properly

If you suddenly discover that one of your programs will not open or run properly, it could be the result of a software conflict. Occasionally—for some unknown reason—certain programs cannot coexist peacefully on the same computer. In that case, there are some remedies you can try.

Download a Newer Version

Many companies release new versions of their software on a regular basis that offer improved features and resolve problems that were discovered in the previous versions. To update a program:

1. If you can successfully open the troubled program, search for an option with a name like Check for Updates. Usually this can be found in one of the drop-down menus located at the top of the program.

2. If you find this option, you must connect to the Internet so the program can update itself.

3. If you can't update the program, or if the update doesn't resolve your problem, check the program manufacturer's website to see if a newer version is available. If you own a legal copy of the software, you may be able to download the newest version for free.

Download a Patch

Often companies offer small patches that can be downloaded from their websites to fix problems or glitches in their software. To locate and download a software patch:

1. Connect to the Internet and visit the website for the program's manufacturer.

2. Near the top of the website's main page, search for a link with a name like Support or Customer Service.

3. After clicking this link, look for a section labeled Updates or Downloads.

Temporarily Disable Anti-Virus or Anti-Spyware Software

Although anti-virus and anti-spyware software are essential for the protection and security of your computer, sometimes they can interfere with the actions of other programs. If updating or patching your troubled program doesn't solve its problems, try temporarily disabling or shutting down your anti-virus and/or anti-spyware software. Here's how:

1. If you are connected to the Internet, disconnect from it. For users of dial-up services like AOL, MSN, or Earthlink, this is done simply by logging off your Internet service. For users of high-speed Internet (DSL or cable), this is done by engaging the Internet lock feature of your software firewall or by unplugging the Ethernet cable from the back of your computer.

2. Right-click the icon for your anti-virus or anti-spyware program, which is usually located in the lower-right corner of Windows near the clock.

3. Select the option to Close or Disable or Shut Down.

4. Restart your troubled program to see if it works properly. If it does, keep your anti-virus or anti-spyware program turned off until you are finished using the troubled program.

5. When you are ready to resume normal computer activities like using email or surfing the Internet, remember to turn on your anti-virus software by right-clicking its icon near the Windows clock and selecting Enable or Restore. You should always have your anti-virus and anti-spyware software turned on when connected to the Internet. If the anti-virus icon is not there, you must manually restart the program by doing the following:

    a. Click the Start button in the lower-left corner of Windows.

    b. Click All Programs.

    c. Select the folder containing the name of your anti-virus software. For example, if you use CA Anti-Virus, select the folder labeled CA.

    d. Click the shortcut to launch the program.

10

CUSTOMIZING WINDOWS FOR YOUR PERSONAL PREFERENCES

C ertain features of Windows XP may not be set to your liking. To customize Windows to meet your personal preferences, follow the tips in this chapter.

Prevent Windows Messenger from Loading

The popularity of instant-messaging (IM) software has soared in recent years. Built into Windows XP is an IM program called Windows Messenger that by default loads when Windows starts. You can prevent it from loading when Windows starts, as follows:

1. Open Windows Messenger by double-clicking its icon located in the lower-right corner of Windows.

2. Click the Tools drop-down menu.

3. Select Options.

4. A window opens. Click the Preferences tab.

5. Under the General heading, remove the checkmark from the Run Windows Messenger When Windows Starts box. Next, remove the checkmark from the Allow Windows Messenger to Run in the Background box (see Figure 10-1).

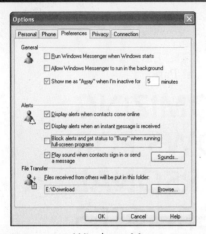

Figure 10-1: Windows Messenger options

6. Click the OK button.

7. Close Windows Messenger, and then open Outlook Express.

8. Click the Tools drop-down menu.

9. Select Options.

10. A window opens. Under the General tab, remove the checkmark from the Automatically Log On to Windows Messenger box.

11. Click the Apply button.

12. Click the OK button.

Hide or Disable Windows Messenger

Even if you tweak Windows Messenger so that it no longer loads when your computer starts, there are still some occasions when it may load anyway. If so, you can hide or disable it. There are a few different ways to do this, each of which is equally effective.

Remove Windows Messenger from the Start Menu

This quick fix hides Windows Messenger from sight by removing it from the Start menu. However, no changes are actually made to Messenger, so it remains intact and can be manually located and opened at any time. Follow these steps:

1. Click the Start button in the lower-left corner of Windows.

2. Click the Control Panel. (If you don't see this option, your Start menu is in classic mode. In that case, click Settings, and then select the Control Panel.)

3. Double-click Add or Remove Programs.

4. A window opens. In the left window pane, click the Add/Remove Windows Components icon.

5. A new window opens. Using the scroll bar on the right, scroll down and locate Windows Messenger. Next to it, remove the checkmark from the box (see Figure 10-2).

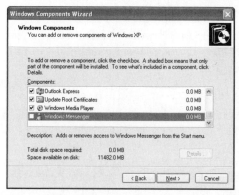

Figure 10-2: Removing Windows Messenger from the Start menu

6. Click the Next button.

7. Windows begins the process of hiding Messenger from the Start menu, which could take a minute or two. When it has completed, click the Finish button.

8. Exit the Add/Remove window by clicking the X button in the upper-right corner.

9. Although Windows Messenger is now hidden, its shortcut may linger in the lower-right corner of Windows (near the clock). To make this shortcut disappear, right-click it and select Exit.

10. If you change your mind and want to use Windows Messenger again, simply repeat these steps, but this time put a checkmark in the Windows Messenger box.

Rename Windows Messenger's Folder

Another way to disable Messenger is to rename its folder, which prevents Windows from locating it. Although this fix is very rudimentary,

it successfully stops Messenger from launching. To use this fix, follow
these steps:

1. Double-click the My Computer icon on your desktop. If this
   icon is not available, click the Start button in the lower-left
   corner of Windows and click My Computer. If you can't
   find the My Computer icon anywhere, do the following:

   a. Right-click in the empty space on your desktop.

   b. Select Properties.

   c. A window will open. Click the Desktop tab.

   d. Near the bottom of the window, click the Customize
      Desktop button.

   e. Another window opens. On the General tab, beneath
      the words Desktop Icons, place a checkmark in the
      My Computer box.

   f. Click the OK button.

   g. You will be returned to the previous screen. Click the
      Apply button.

   h. Click the OK button.

   i. The My Computer icon appears on your desktop.
      Double-click it.

2. A window opens. Double-click the icon for your C: drive
   (unless you installed Windows in a different location, in
   which case you would double-click that drive letter).

3. Double-click the Program Files folder.

4. Locate the Messenger folder and right-click it.

5. Select Rename.

6. Give the folder a name that is easily recognizable, such as
   MessengerDisabled.

7. If you change your mind and want to use Windows
   Messenger again, simply rename this folder Messenger.

Force Windows to Use a Different
Instant Messenger

Instead of hiding or removing Windows Messenger, you can change
the settings in Windows so that it recognizes another program as

your default instant messenger. The advantage of this is that it keeps Windows Messenger intact and ready to use whenever you want it.

Note

This option works only on Windows XP computers that have a minimum of Service Pack 1 installed.

To designate a different instant messaging program:

1. Click the Start button in the lower-left corner of Windows.

2. Click the Control Panel. (If you don't see this option, your Start menu is in classic mode. In that case, click Settings, and then select the Control Panel.)

3. Double-click Add or Remove Programs.

4. A window opens. In the left window pane, click the Set Program Access and Defaults icon.

5. Click the Custom button.

6. Scroll down until you see the Choose a Default Instant Messaging Program heading. Click the Use My Current Instant Messaging Program button. Next, put a checkmark in the Enable Access to This Program box (see Figure 10-3).

7. Click the OK button.

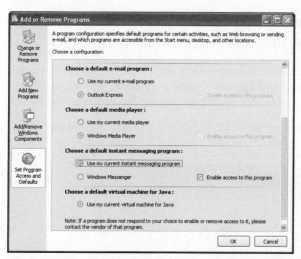

Figure 10-3: Forcing Windows to use a different instant messenger

Change the Windows Registration Name

If you bought a previously owned computer, there is a good chance that Windows still says it is registered to its former owner. To remove that name and insert your own, you must edit the Windows registry:

Warning

Be careful when editing the registry. Deleting or editing the wrong entries could cause more problems.

1. Click the Start button in the lower-left corner of Windows.

2. Click Run.

3. A window will appear. Type **regedit** in the blank, and then click the OK button or press the Enter key.

4. The Windows Registry Editor opens. In the left window pane, double-click the HKEY_LOCAL_MACHINE registry key. If you can't find it, do the following:

   a. In the left window pane of the Registry Editor, scroll to the top.

   b. If any of the HKEY registry keys are open — as indicated by a minus sign (-) on their left side — close them by clicking that minus sign. When a registry key has been properly closed, it will have a plus sign (+) next to it.

   c. Repeat this process for the remaining HKEY registry keys until the only things visible in the left window pane are the five HKEY keys (see Figure 10-4).

   d. Double-click the HKEY_LOCAL_MACHINE registry key.

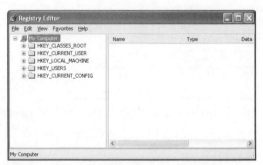

Figure 10-4: Selecting the HKEY_LOCAL MACHINE registry key

5. A new column of registry keys appears. Double-click Software.

6. A long column of registry keys will appear. Scroll down until you find Microsoft, and then double-click it.

7. Another long list of registry keys appears. Scroll down and double-click Windows NT.

8. Click the CurrentVersion registry key.

9. In the right window pane, double-click the RegisteredOwner registry value (see Figure 10-5).

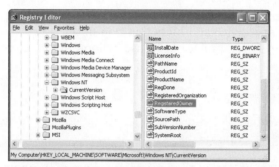

Figure 10-5: Accessing the RegisteredOwner registry value

10. A window opens. Under the Value Data heading is the name of the previous owner. Delete it, and then type your name in the blank.

11. Click the OK button.

12. Above RegisteredOwner, double-click the registry value named RegisteredOrganization (see Figure 10-6).

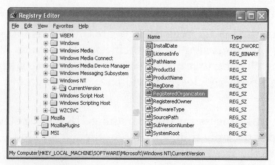

Figure 10-6: Accessing the RegisteredOrganization registry value

13. Under the Value Data heading is the name of the previous owner's employer or organization. Delete it, and then type the name of your organization (or you can just leave it blank if you want).

14. Click the OK button.

15. Exit the Registry Editor by clicking the X button in the upper-right corner.

Pop the Balloon Tips

To make your computer easier to use, Windows XP often displays *balloon tips*, which are advice and hints that pop up for a few seconds and then disappear. If you prefer not to use balloon tips, you can disable them:

Warning
Be careful when editing the registry. Deleting or editing the wrong entries could cause more problems.

1. Click the Start button in the lower-left corner of Windows.

2. Click Run.

3. A window appears. Type **regedit** in the blank, and then click the OK button or press Enter.

4. The Windows Registry Editor will open. In the left window pane, double-click the HKEY_CURRENT_USER registry key. If you can't find it, do the following:

   a. In the left window pane of the Registry Editor, scroll to the top.

   b. If any of the HKEY registry keys are open — as indicated by a minus sign (-) on their left side — close them by clicking that minus sign. When a registry key has been properly closed, it will have a plus sign (+) next to it.

   c. Repeat this process for the remaining HKEY registry keys until the only things visible in the left window pane are the five HKEY keys (see Figure 10-7).

   d. Double-click the HKEY_CURRENT_USER registry key.

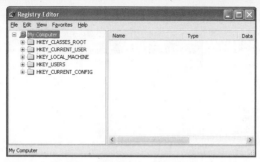

Figure 10-7: Five HKEY registry keys

5. A new column of registry keys appears. Double-click Software.

6. A long column of registry keys appears. Scroll down until you find Microsoft, and then double-click it.

7. Another long list of registry keys appears. Scroll down and double-click Windows.

8. Double-click the CurrentVersion registry key.

9. Double-click the Explorer registry key.

10. Click the Advanced registry key (see Figure 10-8).

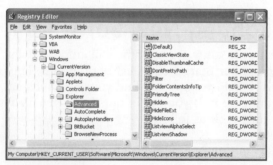

Figure 10-8: Accessing the Advanced registry key

11. Click the Edit drop-down menu located in the upper-left corner of the Windows Registry Editor.

12. Select New.

13. Select DWORD Value.

14. In the right window pane, a new registry value appears. Rename it EnableBalloonTips (see Figure 10-9).

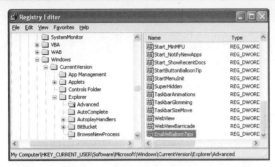

Figure 10-9: Renaming the registry value

15. After renaming the value, double-click it to open it.

16. Under the Value Data heading, make sure there is a 0.

17. Click the OK button.

18. Exit the Registry Editor by clicking the X button in the upper-right corner.

19. If you change your mind and want to allow the balloon tips to appear, all you have to do is repeat these steps to locate the EnableBalloonTips registry key. Open it, delete the 0, and type **1** in its place.

Stop Highlighting New Software

Whenever you install new software, its name will automatically become highlighted in your Start menu's list of programs. The purpose of doing this is to help you quickly find your new software in case you need to configure it. If you prefer not to see this highlighting, you can easily turn it off as follows:

1. Click the Start button in the lower-left corner of Windows.

2. Click the Control Panel. (If you don't see this option, your Start menu is in classic mode. In that case, click Settings, and then select the Control Panel.)

3. If the Control Panel is in category view, click the Appearance and Themes category, and then click the Taskbar and Start Menu icon. If the Control Panel is in classic view, simply double-click the Taskbar and Start Menu icon.

4. A window opens. Click the Start Menu tab.

5. Click the Customize button.

6. Another window opens. Click the Advanced tab.

7. Under the Start Menu Settings heading, remove the check-mark from the Highlight Newly Installed Programs box.

8. Click the OK button.

9. You are returned to the previous window. Click the Apply button.

10. Click the OK button.

Turn Off Error Reporting

When Windows XP crashes or hits a snag, it usually displays an error message and asks for permission to report the problem to Microsoft via the Internet. To prevent these messages from appearing, turn off the error-reporting feature:

1. Right-click the My Computer icon on your desktop. If this icon is not available, click the Start button in the lower-left corner of Windows and right-click My Computer. If you can't find the My Computer icon anywhere, do the following:

    a. Right-click in the empty space on your desktop.

    b. Select Properties.

    c. A window opens. Click the Desktop tab.

    d. Near the bottom of the window, click the Customize Desktop button.

    e. Another window will open. On the General tab, beneath the words Desktop Icons, place a checkmark in the My Computer box.

    f. Click the OK button.

    g. You are returned to the previous screen. Click the Apply button.

    h. Click the OK button.

    i. The My Computer icon appears on your desktop. Double-click it.

2. Select Properties.

3. A window opens. Click the Advanced tab.

4. Click the Error Reporting button located in the lower-right corner of this window.

5. Select the option to Disable Error Reporting. If you still want to be notified when serious errors occur, put a checkmark in the But Notify Me When Critical Errors Occur box. If you want to disable all types of error reporting so that you never see any error messages, remove the checkmark from this box.

Disable Step-by-Step Searches

Windows has an internal search companion that enables you to quickly locate files, folders, or programs on your computer. By default, this search engine takes you through a step-by-step process designed to refine your searches and make them more successful. Some computer users prefer to disable this feature to make their searches more streamlined and fast. Here's how:

1. Click the Start button in the lower-left corner of Windows.

2. Click Search.

3. The Windows Search Companion opens. Use the scroll bar to locate Change Preferences, and then click it.

4. Scroll down and click Change Files and Folders Search Behavior.

5. Click the Advanced button.

6. Click the OK button.

Disable the Search Characters

Another aspect of the Search Companion is the animated characters that provide entertainment during your searches. If you prefer, you can disable these characters:

1. Click the Start button in the lower-left corner of Windows.

2. Click Search.

3. The Windows Search Companion opens. Use the scroll bar to locate Change Preferences, and then click it.

4. Click the Without an Animated Screen Character option. The character will make a humorous exit and disappear.

5. If you change your mind and want to bring back the animated character, follow the previous steps, but this time click With an Animated Screen Character.

Show Inactive Icons

If you have a large number of programs installed on your computer, you might have noticed that the right corner of Windows is jam-packed with icons that are actually shortcuts to your programs. To keep this area clean, Windows XP automatically hides the icons for any programs that have not been used recently. If you prefer to have these icons remain visible at all times, you must disable the feature known as Hide Inactive Icons. Here's how:

1. Click the Start button in the lower-left corner of Windows.

2. Click the Control Panel. (If you don't see this option, your Start menu is in classic mode. In that case, click Settings, and then select the Control Panel.)

3. If the Control Panel is in category view, click the Appearance and Themes category, and then click the Taskbar and Start Menu icon. If the Control Panel is in classic view, simply double-click the Taskbar and Start Menu icon.

4. A window opens. Click the Taskbar tab.

5. Remove the checkmark from the Hide Inactive Icons box.

6. Click the Apply button.

7. Click the OK button.

Re-Sync the Windows Clock

If the clock in the lower-right corner of Windows ever displays the wrong time, you can synchronize it with an atomic clock on the Internet—which will ensure that your computer displays the precise time every time.

Note

This feature is not available on computers that belong to a network "domain" (usually domains are found in offices or other business settings).

To reset your clock:

1. Connect to the Internet.

2. Double-click the clock located in the lower-right corner of Windows. The Date and Time Properties window opens, displaying a clock and a calendar.

3. Click the Internet Time tab.

4. Make sure there is a checkmark in the Automatically Synchronize with an Internet Time Server box. If it is missing, restore the checkmark by clicking the box.

5. Click the Update Now button. Windows attempts to synchronize your clock with an Internet time server. If successful, this results in your computer receiving the accurate time. If it is not successful, then it is possible that it is receiving interference from another program like a software firewall. In that case, do the following:

   a. Temporarily disable your firewall.

   b. Repeat the steps to synchronize your clock.

   c. Be sure to enable your firewall after you have completed these steps.

If this does the trick, consult your firewall's help menu or contact its manufacturer for assistance in tweaking the firewall to give the Windows clock permission to access the Internet.

Disable Automatic Cleanup of Your Desktop

To keep your desktop free of clutter, Windows XP offers to automatically relocate any shortcuts that haven't been used in quite a while. If you are satisfied with the layout of your desktop and don't want it changed, you should disable the Desktop Cleanup Wizard, like this:

1. Right-click in the empty space on your desktop.

2. Select Properties.

3. A window opens. Click the Desktop tab.

4. Click the Customize Desktop button located in the lower-left corner.

5. Remove the checkmark from the Run Desktop Cleanup Wizard Every 60 Days box.

6. Click the OK button.

Adjust AutoPlay

When you insert a CD or DVD disc into your computer, the Windows AutoPlay feature springs into action and opens, plays, or displays the files on the disc. To adjust the AutoPlay settings, do the following:

1. Double-click the My Computer icon on your desktop. If this icon is not available, click the Start button in the lower-left corner of Windows and click My Computer. If you can't find the My Computer icon anywhere, do the following:

   a. Right-click in the empty space on your desktop.

   b. Select Properties.

   c. A window opens. Click the Desktop tab.

   d. Near the bottom of the window, click the Customize Desktop button.

   e. Another window opens. On the General tab, beneath Desktop Icons, place a checkmark in the My Computer box.

   f. Click the OK button.

   g. You will be returned to the previous screen. Click the Apply button.

   h. Click the OK button.

   i. The My Computer icon appears on your desktop. Double-click it.

2. A window opens. Right-click the icon for your CD/DVD burner or other media device.

3. Select Properties.

4. A window opens. Click the AutoPlay tab.

5. You will see a drop-down menu that allows you to choose between seven categories: Music Files, Pictures, Video Files, Mixed Content, Music CD, DVD Movie, and Blank CD (see Figure 10-10). Use this menu to select one of the categories, and then go to the Actions heading below it.

Figure 10-10: Windows AutoPlay properties

6. If you want AutoPlay to ask you what to do each time a disc is inserted into your CD or DVD drive, click the Prompt Me Each Time to Choose an Action button. If you want AutoPlay to automatically perform a specific action each time a disc is inserted, click the Select an Action to Perform button. Next, select one of the options below it. For example, if you want a CD full of digital photos to automatically appear as a slideshow, do the following:

    a. Click the drop-down menu and select Pictures.

    b. Click Select an Action to Perform.

    c. Click View a Slideshow of the Images.

There are numerous combinations to choose, so spend time deciding how best to customize AutoPlay to suit your needs.

7. When you are finished configuring AutoPlay, click the Apply button.

8. Click the OK button.

Repair AutoPlay

If AutoPlay isn't working like it should, it might have been turned off accidentally. Before repairing AutoPlay, follow the steps in the next section "Disable AutoPlay" to see if any of the AutoPlay categories have been set to Take No Action. However, if the problem continues you can fix it by editing the Windows registry, like this:

Warning

Be careful when editing the registry. Deleting or editing the wrong entries could cause more problems.

1. Click the Start button in the lower-left corner of Windows.

2. Click Run.

3. A window opens. Type **regedit** in the blank, and then click the OK button or press the Enter key.

4. The Windows Registry Editor will open. In the left window pane, double-click the HKEY_LOCAL_MACHINE registry key. If you can't find it, do the following:

   a. In the left window pane of the Registry Editor, scroll to the top.

   b. If any of the HKEY registry keys are open — as indicated by a minus sign (-) on their left side — close them by clicking that minus sign. When a registry key has been properly closed, it will have a plus sign (+) next to it.

   c. Repeat this process for the remaining HKEY registry keys until the only things visible in the left window pane are the five HKEY keys (see Figure 10-11).

   d. Double-click the HKEY_LOCAL_MACHINE registry key.

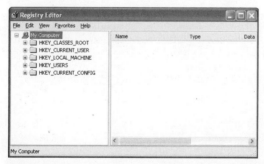

Figure 10-11: Accessing the HKEY_LOCAL_MACHINE registry key

5. A new column of registry keys appears. Double-click System.

6. Another column of registry keys appears. Double-click CurrentControlSet.

7. Double-click the Services registry key.

8. A long list of registry keys will appear. Scroll down and click Cdrom (see Figure 10-12).

Figure 10-12: Accessing the Cdrom registry key

9. In the right window pane, look for a registry value labeled AutoRun (see Figure 10-13). If it is there, proceed to Step 10. If you do not have this registry value, then you need to create it, like this:

    a. Click the Edit drop-down menu located at the top of the Windows Registry Editor.

    b. Select New.

    c. Select DWORD Value.

    d. In the right window pane, a new registry value will appear. Rename it AutoRun (make sure it looks exactly like Figure 10-13).

Figure 10-13: Renaming the registry key

10. Double-click the AutoRun value.

11. A window opens. Under the Value Data heading, delete any number you see and type 1 in its place.

12. Click the OK button.

13. Exit the Registry Editor by clicking the X button in the upper-right corner.

Disable AutoPlay

Some people prefer to have Windows take no action when they insert a disc into their CD or DVD drive. If you want to disable AutoPlay, you have a few options.

For Windows XP Home Edition:

1. Double-click the My Computer icon on your desktop. If this icon is not available, click the Start button in the lower-left corner of Windows and click My Computer. If you can't find the My Computer icon anywhere, do the following:

   a. Right-click in the empty space on your desktop.

   b. Select Properties.

   c. A window opens. Click the Desktop tab.

   d. Near the bottom of the window, click the Customize Desktop button.

   e. Another window opens. On the General tab, beneath Desktop Icons, place a checkmark in the My Computer box.

   f. Click the OK button.

   g. You are returned to the previous screen. Click the Apply button.

   h. Click the OK button.

   i. The My Computer icon appears on your desktop. Double-click it.

2. A window opens. Right-click the icon for your CD/DVD burner or other media device.

3. Select Properties.

4. A window opens. Click the AutoPlay tab.

5. A drop-down menu appears that allows you to choose between seven categories: Music Files, Pictures, Video Files, Mixed Content, Music CD, DVD Movie, and Blank CD. Use this menu to select one of the categories.

6. Under the Actions heading, click the Select an Action to Perform button.

7. Click Take No Action.

8. Repeat this process for each of the seven categories.

9. When you are finished, click the Apply button.

10. Click the OK button.

For Windows XP Professional Edition:

1. Click the Start button in the lower-left corner of Windows.

2. Click Run.

3. A window opens. Type **gpedit.msc** in the blank, and then click the OK button or press the Enter key.

4. The Group Policy window will open. In the left window pane, below the words Computer Configuration, double-click the Administrative Templates folder.

5. Single-click the System folder.

6. In the right window pane, double-click Turn Off AutoPlay.

7. Another window opens. Under the Setting tab is a Turn Off AutoPlay heading. Beneath it, click the Enabled button (see Figure 10-14).

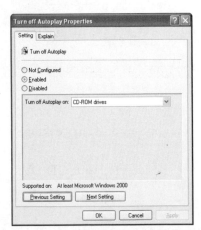

Figure 10-14: Disabling AutoPlay

8. A drop-down menu appears in the center of the window. Click it, and then choose either to turn off AutoPlay only for the CD-ROM drives or for all drives.

9. Click the Apply button.

10. Click the OK button.

11. Shut down your computer and restart it.

11

FIX INTERNET ISSUES

One day your Internet is sailing smoothly. The next day it is dead in the water. Sound familiar? From connection difficulties to broken downloads, Internet issues are some of the most common problems. In addition to tuning your PC with CA's PC Pitstop Optimize software, learn how to fix Internet issues in this chapter.

Repair a Broken Internet Connection

A common problem experienced by Windows XP users is a malfunctioning Internet connection. There are several reasons why this occurs — and just as many remedies.

Temporarily Disable Your Software Firewall

Sometimes a software firewall can experience a digital "hiccup" that interferes with the way it monitors and manages your Internet connection. Common symptoms of this problem include a suddenly slow Internet connection, web pages that stall or are unresponsive, or the complete inability to access the Internet. To determine if your firewall is the cause of your problems, you can temporarily disable it as follows:

1. Right-click the icon for your firewall, which is usually located in the lower-right corner of Windows near the clock.

2. Select the option to disable the firewall. If not available open the actual program and disable it. If you need assistance refer to the product help or documentation.

3. Try connecting to the Internet. If you are successful, restart your firewall by right-clicking its icon near the Windows clock and selecting Enable or Restore. If the firewall's icon is not there, then you must manually restart the program by doing the following:

   a. Click the Start button in the lower-left corner of Windows.

   b. Click All Programs.

   c. Select the folder containing the name of your firewall software. For example, if you use CA Personal Firewall, select the CA folder.

   d. Click the shortcut to launch the program.

Reboot Your Modem, Your Router, or Both

Sometimes a malfunctioning Internet connection can be caused by an error in computer hardware such as a cable or DSL modem or a router. To correct any problems with these devices, you must reboot them as follows:

1. Shut down your computer.

2. Unplug the power cord from the back of your modem and router. An alternative method is to use the tip of a pencil to push the small reset button located at the rear of the modem or router.

3. The lights on the front of your modem or router go dark. Wait 30 seconds, and then plug the power cord back in. This causes the lights on the front of the modem or router to begin blinking rapidly in a particular pattern. Wait for an additional 30 seconds, and then restart your computer.

Use ipconfig

If temporarily disabling your firewall or rebooting your hardware didn't get you back online, there might be a problem with your IP address. To resolve this issue, you must use a program called ipconfig. Here's how:

1. Click the Start button in the lower-left corner of Windows.

2. Click Run.

3. A window will open. Type **cmd** in the blank, and then click the OK button or press the Enter key.

4. A command window opens. Type **ipconfig /flushdns** (see Figure 11-1), and then press the Enter key.

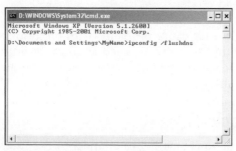

Figure 11-1: Accessing ipconfig

5. Type **ipconfig /release** and press the Enter key.

6. Type **ipconfig /renew** and press the Enter key.

7. Close the command window by clicking the X button in the upper-right corner.

Reinstall TCP/IP

On rare occasions, corruption or damage can occur to the TCP/IP stack, or the section of Windows that handles your Internet connection. The following should fix this problem:

1. Click the Start button in the lower-left corner of Windows.

2. Click Run.

3. A window opens. Type **cmd** in the blank, and then click the OK button or press the Enter key.

4. A command window opens. Type **netsh int ip reset c:\resetlog.txt** (see Figure 11-2) and press the Enter key.

Note

If Windows XP is not installed on your C: drive, you must replace the C: in this command with the correct drive letter followed by a colon.

Figure 11-2: Command window

5. Reinstalling TCP/IP may cause problems with programs that monitor your Internet activity, such as software firewalls. If you experience any problems with these programs you should uninstall them, and then reinstall them.

Repair the Winsock

Another potential cause of your inability to connect to the Internet is a winsock file, a component dealing with your Internet connect settings, that has been altered or damaged by spyware or other digital threats. Fortunately, repairing the winsock is easy to do. The appropriate method of repair depends on whether you have installed a special collection of Windows security patches known as Service Pack 2. Check for it by doing the following:

1. Right-click the My Computer icon on your desktop. If this icon is not available, click the Start button in the lower-left corner of Windows and right-click My Computer. If you can't find the My Computer icon anywhere, do the following:

   a. Right-click in the empty space on your desktop.

   b. Select Properties.

   c. A window opens. Click the Desktop tab.

   d. Near the bottom of the window, click the Customize Desktop button.

   e. Another window opens. On the General tab, beneath Desktop Icons, place a checkmark next to My Computer.

   f. Click the OK button.

   g. You are returned to the previous screen. Click the Apply button.

   h. Click the OK button.

   i. The My Computer icon appears on your desktop. Double-click it.

2. Select Properties.

3. A window opens. Under the tab labeled General, look for System. Beneath it, you should see some words identifying your version of Windows as well as any service packs that are installed. To repair the winsock, try the fixes in the following sections that correspond to the type of service pack you have (if any).

To repair the winsock if you have no Service Packs or have Service Pack 1:

1. Click the Start button in the lower-left corner of Windows.

2. Click Run.

3. A window opens. Type **regedit** in the blank, and then click the OK button or press the Enter key.

Warning

Be careful when editing the registry. Deleting or editing the wrong entries could cause more problems.

4. The Windows Registry Editor opens. In the left window pane, double-click the HKEY_LOCAL_MACHINE registry key. If you can't find it, do the following:

   a. In the left window pane of the Registry Editor, scroll to the top.

   b. If any of the HKEY registry keys are open — as indicated by a minus sign (-) on their left side — close them by clicking that minus sign. When a registry key has been properly closed, it will have a plus sign (+) next to it.

   c. Repeat this process for the remaining HKEY registry keys until the only things visible in the left window pane are the five HKEY keys (see Figure 11-3).

   d. Double-click the HKEY_LOCAL_MACHINE registry key.

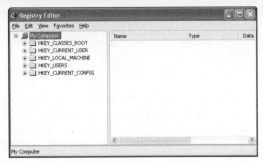

Figure 11-3: Five HKEY registry keys

5. A new column of registry keys appears. Double-click System.

6. Another column of registry keys appears. Double-click CurrentControlSet.

7. Double-click Services.

8. A long list of registry keys appears. Scroll down until you see Winsock (see Figure 11-4), and then right-click it and select Delete.

Figure 11-4: Deleting the Winsock registry key

9. You are asked to confirm the deletion. Click the Yes button.

10. Repeat this procedure to delete the Winsock2 registry key.

11. Exit the Registry Editor by clicking the X button in the upper-right corner.

12. Shut down your computer and restart it.

13. After returning to Windows, click the Start button in the lower-left corner.

14. Click the Control Panel. (If you don't see this option, your Start menu is in classic mode. In that case, click Settings, and then select the Control Panel.)

15. If the Control Panel is in category view, click the Network and Internet Connections category, and then click the Network Connections icon. If the Control Panel is in classic view, simply double-click the Network Connections icon.

16. In the right window pane, right-click the name of your network connection.

17. Select Properties.

18. A window opens. Click the Install button (see Figure 11-5).

Figure 11-5: Network Connection Properties

19. Another window opens. Click the Protocol icon, and then click the Add button.

20. Under the Network Protocol heading, click Microsoft IPv6 Developer Edition (unless your version of Windows is configured differently, in which case you might see the words Microsoft TCP/IP version 6).

21. Click the Have Disk button.

22. Another window opens. In the box below Copy Manufacturer's Files From, type **C:\Windows\inf** (unless Windows XP is installed in another location, in which case, replace C: with a different drive letter followed by a colon). See Figure 11-6.

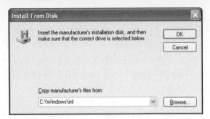

Figure 11-6: Specifying a location

23. Click the OK button.

24. A new window opens. Under the Network Protocol heading, click Internet Protocol (TCP/IP), and then click the OK button.

25. A moment later, you are returned to one of the previous windows. Click the Close button.

26. Shut down your computer and restart it.

To repair the winsock if you have Service Pack 2:

1. Click the Start button in the lower-left corner of Windows.

2. Click Run.

3. A window opens. Type **cmd** in the blank, and then click the button labeled OK or press the Enter key.

4. A command window opens. Type **netsh winsock reset** (see Figure 11-7), and then press the Enter key. This restores your winsock to its original, default configuration.

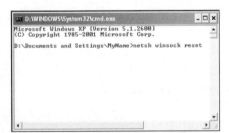

Figure 11-7: Command window

5. Shut down your computer and restart it.

6. Repairing the winsock may cause problems with programs that monitor your Internet activity, such as software firewalls. If you experience any problems with these programs you should uninstall them, and then reinstall them.

Use the System File Checker

Yet another possible cause of your Internet woes is corruption that has occurred in Windows' critical system files. By using a program called System File Checker, you can search for and automatically repair any of these damaged files. Here's how:

1. Click the Start button in the lower-left corner of Windows.

2. Click Run.

3. A window opens. Type **sfc /scanow** in the blank (see Figure 11-8), and then click the OK button or press the Enter key.

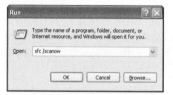

Figure 11-8: Accessing the System File Checker

4. Windows scans your computer to determine whether or not your system files are corrupted. If any files need to be replaced, a message may pop up and ask you to insert your Windows XP CD-ROM. Follow the on-screen instructions.

5. If repairs are made, your damaged files may be overwritten by older versions. As a result, some recent security updates and patches may no longer work properly. This could make your computer vulnerable to Internet threats like worms and hackers. To restore your protection, visit the Windows Update website to re-download the patches.

Back Up Your Bookmarks

During your many Internet journeys, you have probably collected countless bookmarks that can whisk you away to your favorite websites with one click of the mouse. If your bookmarks are erased, you'll probably have a difficult time finding your way back to some of those sites, so don't take any chances — back up your bookmarks today. Follow these steps:

1. Open Internet Explorer.

2. Click the File drop-down menu.

3. Select Import and Export.

4. The Import/Export Wizard opens. Click the Next button.

5. Select Export Favorites, and then click the Next button.

6. To export all of your bookmark folders, click the Next button. To export only one folder, click its name, and then click Next.

7. Under the Export to a File or Address heading, click the Browse button.

8. A window opens that allows you to choose the location on your computer where your bookmarks will be saved. Click the Save In drop-down menu, and then select a drive or folder.

9. In the box labeled File Name, type a name for your backed-up bookmarks, such as My Bookmarks or Exported Bookmarks.

10. Click the Save button.

11. You are returned to the previous window. Click the Next button.

12. Click the Finish button.

13. Use a backup device like a CD or DVD burner to save a copy of your exported bookmarks.

Restore Missing "Favicons"

Favicons are the small pictures displayed alongside a website's address (see Figure 11-9). When you create a shortcut to a website — known as a bookmark or a favorite — the favicon for that site is attached to the bookmark. Many computer users enjoy having their bookmarks enhanced by the fun, eye-pleasing favicons and are puzzled when the favicons suddenly vanish. The reason for this disappearance is that favicons are stored in your Temporary Internet Files folder. Whenever this folder is automatically or manually emptied, the favicons are deleted along with all of your old Internet files. Unfortunately, this leaves your bookmarks looking rather bland and lifeless. To correct this problem, you can use software programs that will automatically find and replace your missing favicons, or you can replace them manually.

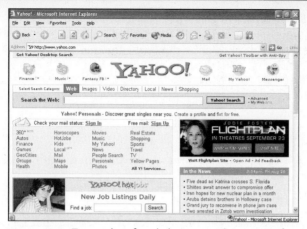

Figure 11-9: Example of web browser showing a favicon

Manually Restore Favicons

If you want to manually select which favicons to restore, follow these steps:

Note

This technique might not work with some websites.

1. Double-click the My Computer icon on your desktop. If this icon is not available, click the Start button in the lower-left corner of Windows and click My Computer. If you can't find the My Computer icon anywhere, do the following:

   a. Right-click in the empty space on your desktop.

   b. Select Properties.

   c. A window opens. Click the Desktop tab.

   d. Near the bottom of the window, click the Customize Desktop button.

   e. Another window opens. On the General tab, beneath Desktop Icons, place a checkmark in the My Computer box.

   f. Click the OK button.

   g. You are returned to the previous screen. Click the Apply button.

   h. Click the OK button.

   i. The My Computer icon appears on your desktop. Double-click it.

2. A window opens. Double-click the icon for your C: drive (unless you have Windows XP installed on a different drive, in which case, double-click the letter for that drive).

3. Click the File drop-down menu located in the upper-left corner.

4. Select New.

5. Select Folder.

6. A new folder appears on your C: drive. Rename this folder Favicons.

7. Open Internet Explorer.

8. In the address bar, type the address of a website that has a favicon you want to capture. For example, type **http://www.yahoo.com** if you want the favicon for Yahoo!.

9. After connecting to the website, click the Tools drop-down menu located at the top of Internet Explorer.

10. Select Internet Options.

11. A window opens. Beneath the Temporary Internet Files heading, click the Settings button.

12. Another window opens. Click the View Files button.

13. A Temporary Internet Files folder opens. At the top of this folder, click the View drop-down menu.

14. Select Details.

15. Scroll through the Temporary Internet Files folder and find the favicon that corresponds to the website you just visited (see Figure 11-10).

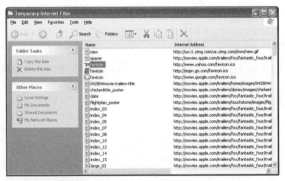

Figure 11-10: Temporary Internet Files folder

16. Right-click the favicon and select Copy.

17. Return to your C: drive.

18. Double-click the Favicons folder you created.

19. Inside this folder, right-click in the empty space and select Paste. This pastes the new favicon into the folder.

20. Return to your C: drive.

21. Double-click the Documents and Settings folder.

22. Double-click the folder containing the name of your Windows account. For example, if your account is named Bob, click the Bob folder.

23. Double-click the Favorites folder.

24. Locate a bookmark you already have that corresponds to the favicon you just copied. For example, if you copied a favicon for Yahoo!, then locate the bookmark for http://www.yahoo.com. If your bookmarks are organized into different folders, you might have to search through them until you find the proper bookmark.

25. Right-click the bookmark and select Properties, which opens the Properties window.

26. Click the Web Document tab.

27. Click the Change Icon button.

28. A new window opens. Click the Browse button that is next to Look for Icons in This File.

29. Another window opens. At the top of it, click the Look in Next drop-down menu, and select your C: drive.

30. Double-click the Favicons folder.

31. Double-click the favicon you copied.

32. You are returned to the previous window. Click the OK button.

33. You are returned to the Properties window. Click the Apply button.

34. Click the OK button. This creates a permanent link between the bookmark and the favicon.

35. To create lasting favicons for all of your favorite websites, repeat this process as many times as necessary.

Prevent Crashes When Copying Text from a Website

Sometimes when you copy a web page and try to paste it into Microsoft Word, the graphics in the web content will cause Word to freeze or crash. To prevent this, try these fixes:

- Do not paste an entire web page into Word.

- Copy small sections of the web page and paste them into Word one by one.

- Do not copy text and web pictures simultaneously.

- If possible, copy and paste each picture or image individually.

- A never-fail alternative is to paste the web content into Notepad, and then transfer it to Word. This option is ideal for large blocks of text. A word of caution: pasting web content into Notepad strips out all pictures, images, and graphics, leaving only plain text. If you're okay with that, follow these steps to transfer web content:

    1. Click the Start button in the lower-left corner of Windows.

    2. Click All Programs.

    3. Select Accessories.

    4. Click Notepad.

    5. Copy the website text and paste it into Notepad, which will strip the text of its web format and convert it to plain text.

    6. Copy the text from Notepad and paste it into Word.

Easily Locate Your Downloads

Have you ever downloaded a program, video, or picture from the Internet but been unable to find where it went? No matter where you search, you just can't seem to locate it. And because you can't remember the name of the download, the Windows Search Companion is useless. This is a common problem for many Internet surfers. A quick, easy solution is to create a special folder on your hard drive that will store all of your downloads. Here's how:

1. Double-click the My Computer icon on your desktop. If this icon is not available, click the Start button in the lower-left corner of Windows and click My Computer. If you can't find the My Computer icon anywhere, do the following:

    a. Right-click in the empty space on your desktop.

    b. Select Properties.

    c. A window opens. Click the Desktop tab.

    d. Near the bottom of the window, click the Customize Desktop button.

    e. Another window opens. On the General tab, beneath Desktop Icons, place a checkmark in the My Computer box.

    f. Click the OK button.

    g. You are returned to the previous screen. Click the Apply button.

    h. Click the OK button.

    i. The My Computer icon appears on your desktop. Double-click it.

2. A window opens. Double-click the icon for your C: drive (unless you installed Windows in a different location, in which case, double-click that drive letter).

3. Click the File drop-down menu.

4. Select New.

5. Select Folder.

6. A new folder (aptly named New Folder) appears in your C: drive. Right-click it, and then select Rename.

7. Type a new name for the folder such as Downloads or My Downloads.

8. Each time you download a new file or program, save it to your new downloads folder so that you always know where to find it.

Reduce the Internet Cache

If you are running out of room on your hard drive, you can free up space by reducing the size of the Internet *cache*, also known as the Temporary Internet Files. This is the place where Internet Explorer stores copies of the images, sounds, and other information related to the websites you have visited recently. The cache actually speeds up your Internet connection by allowing Internet Explorer to view the copies of those web-related files rather than having to retrieve new versions of them from the Internet. However, this feature can also gobble up precious room on a full hard drive. So if creating extra space is your primary concern, you should reduce the size of the cache. Follow these steps:

1. Open Internet Explorer.

2. Click the Tools drop-down menu.

3. Select Internet Options.

4. A window opens. Under the General tab, look for Temporary Internet Files. Click the Settings button.

5. Another window opens. Find the box with a number in it, which is located next to Amount of Disk Space to Use. This number indicates the size of your Internet cache (listed in megabytes). If you are running seriously low on hard drive space, delete the current number, and in its place type a small number like 50 or 25. If you have a bit more room to spare on your hard drive, you can set the cache at a higher number like 250 or 500.

6. Click the OK button.

7. You are returned to the previous window. Click the OK button.

12

ANALYZE YOUR PC

After using CA's PC Pitstop Optimize software, you may find it necessary to make some changes to your PC. Before upgrading your hardware, installing new software, or troubleshooting a computer problem, you need to know certain things about your PC — such as what version of Windows or how much RAM you have. This chapter explains everything you need to know.

Determine Your Version of Windows

Most computer programs and some pieces of hardware have restrictions on what versions of Windows can be used with them. To avoid buying products that won't work with your setup, you should determine what version of Windows you are running.

1. Right-click the My Computer icon on your desktop. If this icon is not available, click the Start button in the lower-left corner of Windows and right-click My Computer. If you can't find the My Computer icon anywhere, do the following:

   a. Right-click in the empty space on your desktop.

   b. Select Properties.

   c. A window opens. Click the Desktop tab.

   d. Near the bottom of the window, click the Customize Desktop button.

e. Another window opens. On the General tab, beneath the words Desktop Icons, place a checkmark in the My Computer box.

f. Click OK.

g. You are returned to the previous screen. Click Apply.

h. Click OK.

i. The My Computer icon appears on your desktop. Right-click it.

2. Select Properties.

3. A window opens. Near the top of it, you should see the version of Windows your computer is running as well as any "service packs" (collections of updates and security patches) that have been installed (see Figure 12-1).

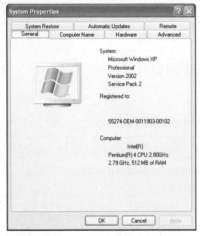

Figure 12-1: System Properties window

Determine Your Version of Internet Explorer

Some software on your computer or certain websites you visit may require you to use a certain version of Internet Explorer in order to function properly (or at all). Here's how to determine what version you have:

1. Double-click the Internet Explorer icon on your desktop. If this icon is not available, click the Start button in the lower-left corner of Windows and click the shortcut labeled either Internet Explorer or Internet.

2. Internet Explorer opens. Click the Help drop-down menu.

3. Click About Internet Explorer.

4. A window opens. Look for the word Version. Listed immediately next to it will be the version number for your copy of Internet Explorer (see Figure 12-2).

Figure 12-2: About Internet Explorer window

5. Click OK.

Determine the Manufacturer and Speed of Your Processor (CPU)

The processor—also known as a CPU—is the part of your computer's hardware that performs the tasks handed out by your software. Typically, the faster a processor is, the more powerful your computer will be. Some programs and newer versions of Windows require a minimum CPU speed in order to work correctly. To find out how fast your CPU is and which company made it, do the following:

1. Right-click the My Computer icon on your desktop. If this icon is not available, click the Start button in the lower-left corner of Windows and right-click My Computer. If you can't find the My Computer icon anywhere, do the following:

    a. Right-click in the empty space on your desktop.

    b. Select Properties.

    c. A window opens. Click the Desktop tab.

    d. Near the bottom of the window, click the Customize Desktop button.

   e. Another window opens. On the General tab, beneath the words Desktop Icons, place a checkmark in the My Computer box.

   f. Click OK.

   g. You are returned to the previous screen. Click Apply.

   h. Click OK.

   i. The My Computer icon appears on your desktop. Right-click it.

2. Select Properties.

3. A window opens. Near the bottom of it, you should see the name of the company that made your CPU (usually it is Intel or AMD) as well as the CPU's speed listed in measurements of "MHz" (megahertz) or "GHz" (gigahertz) — for example, 500 MHz or 1.5 GHz (see Figure 12-3).

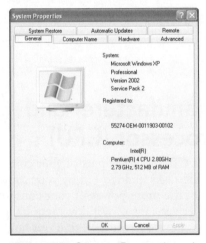

Figure 12-3: System Properties window

Determine Your Amount of System Memory (RAM)

The memory in your computer — commonly referred to as RAM (Random Access Memory) — is the hardware used by Windows and your software to store temporary information. The more RAM you have, the more programs you can use simultaneously and the faster your computer will be. Here's how to find out how much RAM your computer has:

1. Right-click the My Computer icon on your desktop. If this icon is not available, click the Start button in the lower-left corner of Windows and right-click My Computer. If you can't find the My Computer icon anywhere, do the following:

   a. Right-click in the empty space on your desktop.

   b. Select Properties.

   c. A window opens. Click the Desktop tab.

   d. Near the bottom of the window, click the Customize Desktop button.

   e. Another window opens. On the General tab, beneath the words Desktop Icons, place a checkmark in the My Computer box.

   f. Click OK.

   g. You are returned to the previous screen. Click Apply.

   h. Click OK.

   i. The My Computer icon appears on your desktop. Right-click it.

2. Select Properties.

3. A window opens. Near the bottom of it, you should see the amount of system memory (RAM). See Figure 12-4.

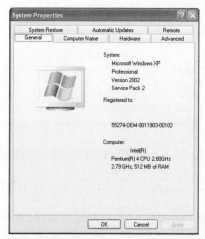

Figure 12-4: System Properties window

Determine Your Hard Drive's Size and Remaining Space

A hard drive is a piece of equipment that stores all of the programs and data on your computer (think of it as a digital warehouse). If your hard drive has too much information on it, your computer can become noticeably slow. If the hard drive becomes completely full, you will be unable to install new programs or download files from the Internet until you free up some space. To determine the overall size of your hard drive and how much room it has left, do the following:

1. Double-click the My Computer icon on your desktop. If this icon is not available, click the Start button in the lower-left corner of Windows and click My Computer. If you can't find the My Computer icon anywhere, do the following:

   a. Right-click in the empty space on your desktop.

   b. Select Properties.

   c. A window opens. Click the Desktop tab.

   d. Near the bottom of the window, click the Customize Desktop button.

   e. Another window opens. On the General tab, beneath the words Desktop Icons, place a checkmark in the My Computer box.

   f. Click OK.

   g. You are returned to the previous screen. Click Apply.

   h. Click OK.

   i. The My Computer icon appears on your desktop. Double-click it.

2. A window opens. Right-click the icon for the hard drive you want to check. For example, if you want to know the size and remaining space for your C: drive (which is the drive that most people have Windows installed on), right-click the icon labeled C:.

3. Select Properties.

4. A window opens. On the General tab, you should see the words Used Space. This indicates how much of your hard drive is being used. You should also see the words Free

Space, which indicates how much room is left on your hard drive (see Figure 12-5). Both of these numbers will be expressed in measurements of gigabytes (GB) or megabytes (MB) — for example, 500MB or 2GB. Don't be alarmed if you see that your gigabytes have a smaller number than your megabytes; a gigabyte is much larger than a megabyte (1 gigabyte is equal to 1,000 megabytes).

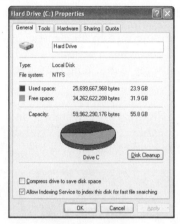

Figure 12-5: Hard Drive Properties window

Open Your Computer's Case

After you have used Windows to do a quick analysis of your PC's primary features, you should open the computer's case and examine the equipment inside. Becoming comfortable with opening the case and identifying the components is essential if you ever want to perform a hardware upgrade on your own.

1. Turn off your computer and unplug it from all electrical outlets. This will prevent you from receiving a serious electrical shock and will protect the computer from being damaged.

2. Examine your case to find out how it opens. Some cases have a removable cover shaped like an upside-down "U" that slides off when some screws are unfastened. Other cases have side panels (or doors) that slide off or swing open when they are unscrewed or when a special button is pressed.

3. If you cannot figure out how to open your computer's case, check the owner's manual or documents that came with your system.

Determine Your Hard Drive's Interface

All hard drives use special data cables to transfer information to and from the rest of your computer. By finding out what type of interface those cables have, you will be able to identify the style of your hard drive (which is crucial if you ever decide to upgrade it to a faster model or add a second one).

1. Turn off your computer and unplug it from all electrical outlets. This will prevent you from receiving a serious electrical shock and will protect the computer from being damaged.

2. Remove the computer's cover.

3. Look for your hard drive (see Figure 12-6), which is one of the few devices that have data cables (also called "ribbon" cables) and power cables connected to them.

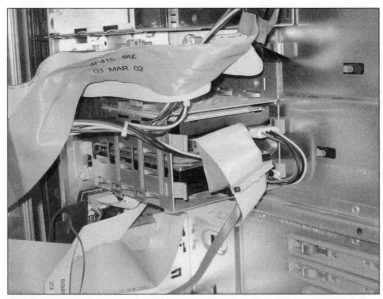

Figure 12-6: Example of hard drive inside your PC

a. If the hard drive has a flat ribbon cable connected to it, you are probably using an IDE or EIDE interface.

b. If the hard drive has a different type of data cable connected to it (like a round one), you are probably using a Serial ATA interface.

Another way to determine your hard drive's interface is to look in the Windows Device Manager.

For Windows 2000 and Windows XP Home/Pro:

1. Right-click the My Computer icon on your desktop. If this icon is not available, click the Start button in the lower-left corner of Windows and right-click My Computer. If you can't find the My Computer icon anywhere, do the following:

    a. Right-click in the empty space on your desktop.

    b. Select Properties.

    c. A window opens. Click the Desktop tab.

    d. Near the bottom of the window, click the Customize Desktop button.

    e. Another window opens. On the General tab, beneath the words Desktop Icons, place a checkmark in the My Computer box.

    f. Click OK.

    g. You are returned to the previous screen. Click Apply.

    h. Click OK.

    i. The My Computer icon appears on your desktop. Right-click it.

2. Select Properties.

3. A window opens. Click the Hardware tab.

4. Click the Device Manager button.

5. Another window opens. Click the plus sign (+) located next to the IDE ATA/ATAPI Controllers category (see Figure 12-7).

6. You will see a list of the hard drive "channels" on your computer. An IDE Channel indicates you are using an IDE hard drive. A Serial ATA Channel indicates you are using a serial ATA hard drive.

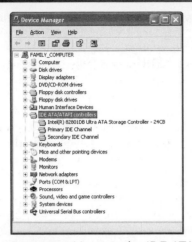

Figure 12-7: Viewing the IDE ATA/ATAPI Controllers category

For Windows 98 and ME:

1. Right-click the My Computer icon on your desktop.

2. Select Properties.

3. A window opens. Click the Device Manager tab.

4. Click the plus sign (+) located next to the Hard Disk Controllers category (see Figure 12-8).

Figure 12-8: Viewing the Hard Disk Controllers category

5. You will see a list of the hard drive "channels" on your computer. An IDE Channel indicates you are using an IDE hard drive. A Serial ATA Channel indicates you are using a serial ATA hard drive.

Look for USB Ports

Most modern computer peripherals such as printers and digital cameras connect to computers through USB ports. Determining whether or not your computer is equipped with USB will tell you what devices and gadgets can be used with your computer.

1. Turn off your computer and unplug it from all electrical outlets. This will prevent you from receiving a serious electrical shock and will protect the computer from being damaged.

2. Pull your computer away from your desk so you can get a good look at its case. On the back of the computer, search for a thin, rectangular connector (see Figure 12-9). That is a USB port, into which you can plug USB devices such as printers, keyboards, mice, digital cameras, and much more.

Figure 12-9: Example of USB ports

3. If you cannot find any USB ports on the back of your computer, look at the front of the case. Some computers have these ports hidden behind doors or panels that swing open (see Figure 12-10).

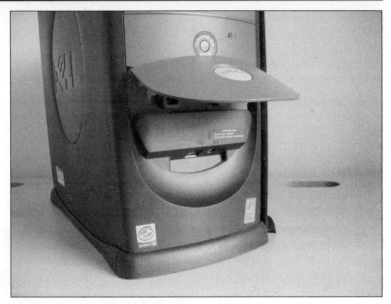

Figure 12-10: Example of USB ports in front

Identify Your Version of USB

There are two versions of USB: 1.1 (somewhat slow) and 2.0 (very fast). Although their speeds are different, both USB formats are compatible with each other (which means you can plug a 1.1 device into a 2.0 port or vice versa). Identifying the speed of the USB ports on your computer can be quite helpful when deciding what type of peripherals to purchase. For example, if your computer has USB 2.0, you should buy a digital camera that also has USB 2.0 so you can transfer photos from the camera to your computer at the highest possible speed. To determine which version of USB you have, use the Windows Device Manager.

Note
Plugging a 1.1 device into a 2.0 port will not make that device perform faster. However, plugging a 2.0 device into a 1.1 port will cause the 2.0 device to perform slower.

For Windows 2000 and Windows XP Home/Pro:

1. Right-click the My Computer icon on your desktop. If this icon is not available, click the Start button in the lower-left corner of Windows and right-click My Computer. If you can't find the My Computer icon anywhere, do the following:

    a. Right-click in the empty space on your desktop.

    b. Select Properties.

    c. A window opens. Click the Desktop tab.

    d. Near the bottom of the window, click the Customize Desktop button.

    e. Another window opens. On the General tab, beneath the words Desktop Icons, place a checkmark in the My Computer box.

    f. Click OK.

    g. You are returned to the previous screen. Click Apply.

    h. Click OK.

    i. The My Computer icon appears on your desktop. Right-click it.

2. Select Properties.

3. A window opens. Click the Hardware tab.

4. Click the Device Manager button.

5. Another window opens. Click the plus sign (+) located next to the Universal Serial Bus Controllers category (see Figure 12-11).

Figure 12-11: Viewing the Universal Serial Bus Controllers category

6. To determine if you have the fastest version of USB (called USB 2.0), look for an "enhanced" USB controller with a name like Standard Enhanced PCI to USB Host Controller, Intel PCI to USB Enhanced Host Controller, or NEC PCI to USB Enhanced Host Controller. If you do not see the word "enhanced," you probably have USB 1.1 (the slower version).

For Windows 98 and ME:

1. Right-click the My Computer icon on your desktop.
2. Select Properties.
3. Click the Device Manager tab.
4. Click the plus sign (+) located next to the Universal Serial Bus Controller category (see Figure 12-12).

Figure 12-12: Viewing the Universal Serial Bus Controller category

5. To determine if you have the fastest version of USB (called USB 2.0), look for an "enhanced" USB controller with a name like Standard Enhanced PCI to USB Host Controller, Intel PCI to USB Enhanced Host Controller, or NEC PCI to USB Enhanced Host Controller. If you do not see the word "enhanced," you probably have USB 1.1 (the slower version).

Look for FireWire Ports

FireWire is another type of connection used to transfer information between a computer and a peripheral such as an external hard drive or a video camera. The speed of FireWire is similar to that of USB 2.0. To discover if your computer is FireWire-capable, do the following:

1. Turn off your computer and unplug it from all electrical outlets. This will prevent you from receiving a serious electrical shock and will protect the computer from being damaged.

2. Pull your computer away from your desk so you can get a good look at its case. On the back of the computer, search for a connector that looks like Figure 12-13. That is a FireWire port, into which you can plug FireWire devices such as digital video cameras, external DVD drives, external hard drives, and much more.

Figure 12-13: Example of FireWire ports

3. If you cannot find any FireWire ports on the back of your computer, look at the front of the case. Some computers have these ports hidden behind doors or panels that swing open.

Identify Your CD or DVD Drive

CD-ROM drives sure have come a long way since their humble beginnings. Now there are recordable and rewritable compact discs (CD-R and CD-RW), as well as their offspring: recordable and rewritable DVDs (DVD-R, DVD-RW, DVD+R, DVD+RW). Once you determine what type of CD or DVD drive is inside your computer, you will know which discs to buy and what software can be used with the drive.

1. Look at the front of your CD or DVD drive. Often there are words or logos that indicate the drive's capabilities or features.

2. If you have a CD drive, you should see a Compact Disc logo.

Note

All CD drives play music CDs and read CD-ROM data discs.

3. If you have a DVD drive, you will probably see a DVD logo.

Note

In addition to reading DVD-ROM data discs and playing DVD movies, a DVD drive is backward compatible with CDs. That means it can play music CDs and read CD-ROM data discs.

4. If you have a CD or DVD burner that can record data onto writable or rewritable CD or DVD discs, that feature should be indicated by a logo labeled RW or Rewritable.

If you do not see any words or logos on the front of your CD or DVD drive, you can search for information about it in the Windows Device Manager.

For Windows 2000 and Windows XP Home/Pro:

1. Right-click the My Computer icon on your desktop. If this icon is not available, click the Start button in the lower-left corner of Windows and right-click My Computer. If you can't find the My Computer icon anywhere, do the following:

   a. Right-click in the empty space on your desktop.

   b. Select Properties.

   c. A window opens. Click the Desktop tab.

   d. Near the bottom of the window, click the Customize Desktop button.

    e. Another window opens. On the General tab, beneath the words Desktop Icons, place a checkmark in the My Computer box.

    f. Click OK.

    g. You are returned to the previous screen. Click Apply.

    h. Click OK.

    i. The My Computer icon appears on your desktop. Right-click it.

2. Select Properties.

3. A window opens. Click the Hardware tab.

4. Click the Device Manager button.

5. Another window opens. Click the plus sign (+) located next to the DVD/CD-ROM Drives category (see Figure 12-14).

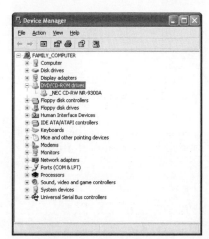

Figure 12-14: Viewing the DVD/CD-ROM Drives category

6. You should see a DVD/CD icon, next to which is the name of your DVD or CD drive as well as its model number. If not, do the following:

    a. Double-click the DVD/CD icon.

    b. A window opens. On the General tab, look for the name and model of you drive.

    c. If you still can't find it, click the Details tab and look there.

For Windows 98 and ME:

1. Right-click the My Computer icon on your desktop.

2. Select Properties.

3. A window opens. Click the Device Manager tab.

4. Click the plus sign (+) located next to the CDROM category (see Figure 12-15).

Figure 12-15: Viewing the CDROM category

5. You should see a CD icon, next to which is the name of your CD or DVD drive as well as its model number. If not, do the following:

    a. Double-click the CD icon.

    b. A window opens. On the General tab, look for the name and model of your drive.

    c. If you still can't find it, click the Details tab and look there.

Look for a Floppy Drive

Although the old-fashioned floppy disk is rarely used anymore, many modern computers still have floppy drives (just in case someone needs to access an old file from 15 years ago that was stored on a floppy). If you aren't sure whether your computer has a floppy drive, do the following:

1. On the front of your computer, look for a slot about three-and-a-half inches long and about half an inch tall (see Figure 12-16).

Figure 12-16: Example of a floppy drive

2. Look for an eject button nearby.

3. Look for an LED status light (which lights up only when the floppy drive is being used).

Look for a Dial-Up Modem

Although the rising popularity of high-speed Internet is gradually pushing slow dial-up Internet services into retirement, most new computers still come equipped with dial-up modems. That way, people have the option to sign up for an inexpensive Internet service in exchange for a slow speed. Here's how you can check for a dial-up modem in your computer:

1. Turn off your computer and unplug it from all electrical outlets. This will prevent you from receiving a serious electrical shock and will protect the computer from being damaged.

2. Pull your computer away from your desk so you can get a good look at its case. On the back of the computer, search for the section that has two telephone jacks (see Figure 12-17). These will be identical to the connectors on a standard telephone as well as the telephone jacks found in the walls of your home or office.

Figure 12-17: Example of a dial-up modem

Look for a Network Card

A network card (also called an Ethernet card) is a device that enables a computer to connect to a high-speed Internet service such as DSL or cable. In addition, some modern computers have Wi-Fi (wireless) cards that allow them to access computer networks and surf the Internet from any room in the house — without using Ethernet cables or connectors. To check for an Ethernet or Wi-Fi card, do the following:

1. Turn off your computer and unplug it from all electrical outlets. This will prevent you from receiving a serious electrical shock and will protect the computer from being damaged.

2. Pull your computer away from your desk so you can get a good look at its case. On the back of the computer, search for an opening that looks like it connects to a very fat telephone cord (see Figure 12-18). This is an Ethernet jack, into which you can connect an Ethernet cable that will deliver high-speed Internet access and connect you to a computer network.

Figure 12-18: Example of a wired network card

3. If the back of your computer has a card with an antenna sticking out of it (see Figure 12-19), you have a wireless (Wi-Fi) network card. You can use it to connect to wireless computer networks and receive wireless high-speed Internet connections.

Figure 12-19: Example of a wireless network card

Identify Your Video Card

Year after year, one of the most popular reasons for using a computer continues to be video games. And with each passing year, the graphics in those games grow more realistic and complex, requiring a powerful video card in order to play properly. To see if your current video card is up to the challenge, compare its specifications to the video game's minimum hardware requirements. In particular, pay attention to the amount of video RAM your card has compared to how much the game requires. Here's how to find your specs.

For all Windows Versions:

1. Right-click in the empty space on your desktop.

2. Select Properties.

3. A window opens. Click the Settings tab.

4. Click the Advanced button.

5. Another window opens. Click the Adapter tab (see Figure 12-20).

6. Based on your version of Windows, you should see a heading called something like Adapter Type. There you will learn the make and model of your video card. You might also see a heading called something like Adapter Information, which will tell you more information about the video card's manufacturer as well as the speed and the amount of RAM the card has.

Figure 12-20: Display Adapter Settings window

Determine the Video Card's Interface

If you want to upgrade to a more powerful video card or replace one that has broken, you need to know what type of interface it uses to connect to your computer.

1. Look for information in the owner's manual or documents that came with your computer. If they are not helpful — or if you have misplaced them — you can inspect the hardware inside your computer to determine which video-card interface you have.

2. Turn off your computer and unplug it from all electrical outlets. This will prevent you from receiving a serious electrical shock and will protect the computer from being damaged.

3. Remove the computer's cover.

4. Locate your video card by following the thick cable that goes from your monitor to the back of your computer. After you have pinpointed your video card, you need to figure out which interface it uses. Here are the three types:

   • **PCI:** This is the traditional interface that has existed in computers for well over a decade. It is used to connect multiple types of hardware such as video cards, sound cards, modems, and more. Usually it has a beige-colored slot that is approximately 3.25 inches wide. Also, most computers have several PCI slots that are stacked in a vertical or horizontal row. So if you see a group of slots neatly lined up, those are probably PCI slots.

   • **AGP:** This interface is used for modern, high-speed video cards. Often it has a brown- or black-colored slot that is nearly 4 inches wide. Most computers have only one AGP slot.

   • **PCI Express (PCIe):** This cutting-edge interface is beginning to appear in new computers. Its slots are noticeably smaller than those belonging to the old-fashioned PCI interface. Unless your computer was made in the past year or so, it is unlikely you have PCI Express.

13

UPGRADE YOUR PC

After using CA's PC Pitstop Optimize software and deciding you need to upgrade your PC, read this chapter to understand how what to upgrade and how to get through the process without any problems.

Have you ever thrown away an automobile because of a flat tire? Of course not. Then why get rid of a computer just because some of its parts have malfunctioned? Much like a car, a computer has many removable parts that can be replaced or upgraded to provide extra speed, power, or storage. Here are the two biggest reasons for upgrading a computer:

- **Saves money:** A new computer usually costs between $500 and $2,000. However, upgrading some of the important parts on a computer can be done for as little as $100. Why is there such a difference? First of all, most new computers come as a complete package, meaning that along with the base unit they include a monitor, keyboard, mouse, and perhaps a printer. If you already have those other items and they are working fine, why replace them? Second, much of the cost of a new computer reflects the time and effort someone spent assembling and configuring it. If you can do the labor yourself, you can save significant dollars. Think of it as a home-improvement project: why hire someone when you can do it yourself?

- **Saves time:** When you buy a new computer, it's like buying a new house — you have to move in all of your belongings and decorate it. In computer terms, that means installing all of your software on the new machine, such as Microsoft Word and other Microsoft Office programs, financial or tax software, video games, and so on; transferring all of your files from your old PC to your new one; setting up your email, Internet, and instant-messaging accounts on your new system; and much more. This process is often very time-consuming and frustrating.

What Should Be Upgraded?

The top questions asked by most digital do-it-yourselfers are "When do I need to upgrade?" and "What parts should be upgraded?" Here are some common PC problems and the hardware or software upgrades that might fix them:

- **Problem:** The computer takes an unusually long time to start up, to shut down, or to open programs and folders. Also, the computer feels sluggish.

  Solution: Upgrade to a faster processor (CPU), or add more system memory (RAM).

- **Problem:** The computer frequently freezes or crashes, often resulting in error messages or blue screens displaying strange text.

  Solution: Update or reinstall Windows, or add more system memory (RAM).

- **Problem:** Messages warn that the computer is running low on disk space or doesn't have enough room to install a program.

  Solution: Upgrade to a larger hard drive, or add a second hard drive.

Upgrade to Windows XP

If you are using an outdated version of Windows such as 95, 98, or ME, consider upgrading to the most recent version. Windows XP or newer operating systems make it much easier to use peripherals such as digital cameras and printers, to connect to wireless networks, and so much more. A newer Windows is usually more stable, and it's usually safer than its predecessors as well.

Here are the basic steps to take when upgrading Windows:

Note

Windows has certain requirements about the type of hardware it can be used with. To see if your computer is compatible with a newer version of Windows follow the steps in Chapter 12 to analyze your PC, and then compare your results to the requirements listed on Windows package.

1. Determine which version of Windows your computer is currently running. For more information, refer to the section "Determine Your Version of Windows" found in Chapter 12.

2. Find out how fast your CPU is and how much RAM you have. For more information, refer to the section "Determine the Manufacturer and Speed of Your Processor (CPU)" and "Determine Your Amount of System Memory (RAM)" found in Chapter 12.

3. Determine how much hard drive space you have left. For more information, refer to the section "Determine Your Hard Drive's Size and Remaining Space" found in Chapter 12.

4. Carefully examine the hardware requirements for the version of Windows you are considering upgrading to because newer versions such as Windows XP require a minimum amount of RAM, hard drive space, and CPU speed in order to function properly.

5. Back up your important files and documents to prevent them from being accidentally damaged or erased when you perform the Windows upgrade. Although such a problem is rare, it is always a good idea to back up your valuable data just to be safe. Backups can be done by using an external hard drive, CD/DVD burner, USB thumbdrive, or tape drive along with backup or burning software.

6. To ensure a successful upgrade, carefully follow the printed instructions — as well as any on-screen instructions — that came with your new version of Windows.

Note

If you are upgrading to a newer Windows from an older model of Windows, you can save a substantial amount of money by purchasing the upgrade version. You do not need to spend the extra money on the "Full" version of XP.

Add More System Memory (RAM)

An inexpensive way to add some zip to your computer is to install more system memory (RAM). Along with the extra speed, you will be able to use more programs at the same time (such as checking email while surfing the Internet while listening to digital music files).

1. Determine what type of RAM your computer uses by reading the owner's manual or documents that came with your system.

2. Purchase a new stick of RAM from a computer or electronics store or from an Internet retailer.

3. Turn off your computer and unplug it from all electrical outlets. This will prevent you from receiving a serious electrical shock and will protect the computer from being damaged.

4. Disconnect all wires and cables from the back of the computer's base unit, and then place the unit on a wooden floor or table. Do not attempt to perform any hands-on computer work while standing or sitting on a carpet or rug. Doing so can generate static electricity that can travel from your body into the computer and damage or destroy your hardware.

5. Remove the computer's cover. For more information, refer to the section "Open Your Computer's Case" in Chapter 12.

6. Locate the memory slots (see Figure 13-1). Typically, there are between two and four of them sitting side by side. To get a clear look at these slots, you might need to move some wires or cables out of the way. If you are simply adding more RAM to your existing RAM, proceed to Step 8. If you are upgrading to a faster type of RAM, you will need to remove your current RAM before you can install the new one (because if fast RAM is mixed with slower RAM, the fast RAM will drop its speed to match that of the slower RAM). For details on removing RAM, proceed to Step 7.

7. To remove a stick of RAM, push down the two small plastic arms that hold the RAM in place. One arm is located on each end of the memory slot and is typically white or beige in color.

8. To install a new stick of RAM, remove it from its protective bag or container. When handling RAM, touch only the smooth sides that do not have circuits printed on them. Do not touch anywhere else, because doing so might damage the RAM.

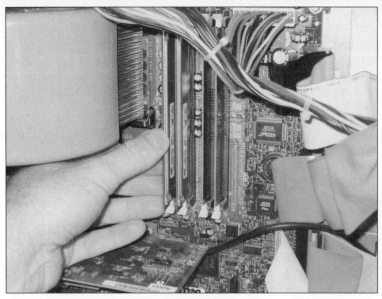

Figure 13-1: Typical empty memory slots

9. Line up the stick of RAM with the memory slot. Both of them are designed so that you can only insert the RAM a certain way. Firmly but gently push the RAM into the slot until both of the slot's plastic arms click into place (see Figure 13-1).

10. If any wires or cables inside the computer were accidentally disconnected while installing the RAM, reconnect them.

11. Close the case, and then return the base unit to your desk.

12. Reconnect the wires and cables into the back of the base unit, and then plug the computer into an electrical outlet and turn it on. When your computer starts, it should instantly recognize the new RAM. If the RAM isn't recognized, your computer most likely will not start at all.

Add an Internal Hard Drive

If your computer is several years old, you probably have a small hard drive that is quickly running out of storage space. Replacing your current hard drive or adding an additional one will give you ample room to store your growing collection of documents, digital photos, digital music, videos, and software.

Note

It is much easier to add a second hard drive than to replace your current one.

1. Find out what type of hard drive your computer uses by referring to the section "Determine Your Hard Drive's Interface" in Chapter 12.

2. Purchase a new hard drive from a computer or electronics store or from an Internet retailer.

3. Turn off your computer and unplug it from all electrical outlets. This will prevent you from receiving a serious electrical shock and will protect the computer from being damaged.

4. Disconnect all wires and cables from the back of the computer's base unit, and then place the unit on a wooden floor or table. Do not attempt to perform any hands-on computer work while standing or sitting on a carpet or rug. Doing so can generate static electricity that can travel from your body into the computer and damage or destroy your hardware.

5. Remove the computer's cover. For more information, refer to the section "Open Your Computer's Case" found in Chapter 12.

6. If your new hard drive is intended to replace your current hard drive, you will need to purchase special software to help you copy all of the files from the old drive to the new one. If your new hard drive is not going to replace your current one but rather is intended to work alongside it and provide extra storage space, proceed to the next step.

7. On the rear of the new hard drive is a tiny plastic "jumper" that must be placed onto the small metal pins in a specific way to allow the drive to work side by side with your current hard drive. On top of most hard drives is a diagram or picture that shows where to place the jumper to make the drive a "slave." Follow these instructions to make your new drive a slave.

8. You probably need to change the jumper settings on your old hard drive so it works properly with the new drive. Look at the diagram or picture on top of the old drive. If you cannot see the picture, you might have to unscrew and remove the drive from your computer. The picture will probably show different jumper settings for "Single" and "Master." Examine the jumper on your old drive. If it is set to "Single," that means it is configured to operate by itself

(without any slave drives). You need to move the jumper to the "Master" position as indicated by the picture.

9. Connect a data cable to the new hard drive. For an EIDE drive, find the ribbon cable connected to your existing hard drive, and then use the gray connector in the middle of it to connect to your new hard drive. For a Serial ATA (SATA) drive, connect the cable that came with the drive to an SATA port on your motherboard.

10. Connect a power cable to the new hard drive. Usually, all computers have extra power cables tucked away inside their cases.

11. Find an empty mounting bay inside the computer's case, and then slide the new hard drive into the bay and secure it (usually by screwing the drive to the case).

12. If any wires or cables inside the computer were accidentally disconnected while installing the new hard drive, reconnect them.

13. Close the case, and then return the base unit to your desk.

14. Reconnect the wires and cables into the back of the base unit, and then plug the computer into an electrical outlet and turn it on. When your computer starts, it should instantly detect your new hard drive.

15. Before you can use the new hard drive, you will probably need to format it. Double-click the My Computer icon on your desktop. If this icon is not available, click the Start button in the lower-left corner of Windows and click My Computer. If you can't find the My Computer icon anywhere, do the following:

    a. Right-click in the empty space on your desktop.

    b. Select Properties.

    c. A window opens. Click the Desktop tab.

    d. Near the bottom of the window, click the Customize Desktop button.

    e. Another window opens. On the General tab, beneath the words Desktop Icons, place a checkmark in the My Computer box.

    f. Click OK.

    g. You will be returned to the previous screen. Click Apply.

   h. Click OK.

   i. The My Computer icon appears on your desktop. Double-click it.

16. A window opens. Right-click the icon for your new hard drive.

17. Select Format.

18. Follow the on-screen instructions to format the drive.

Add an External Hard Drive

The easiest way to add extra storage to your crowded computer is to buy an external hard drive. Basically this device is a standard hard drive enclosed in a rugged plastic or metal case that protects it from being damaged. The best thing is that it connects to your computer through USB or FireWire ports — which means you don't have to open your computer's case and tinker with its internal components.

1. Purchase an external hard drive from a computer or electronics store or from an Internet retailer.

2. If the external hard drive has a USB connector, simply connect one end of the USB cable to the drive and the other end to a USB port on your computer (see Figure 13-2). If the external hard drive has a FireWire connector, simply connect one end of the FireWire cable to the drive and the other end to a FireWire port on your computer.

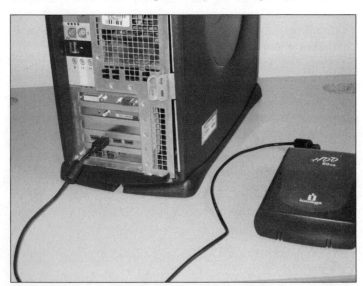

Figure 13-2: Connection of external hard drive

3. Connect the power cable to the external hard drive, and then plug it into an electrical outlet.

4. Windows should automatically detect the external hard drive and enable you to use it right away.

Note
To protect your critical documents from being lost forever as a result of a hard-drive crash, use an external hard drive and backup software to make a copy of your data.

Add a USB Card

USB is the type of connection used by almost all computer peripherals including printers, digital cameras, and scanners. If you have an older computer that lacks USB ports — or if you need extra ports — you can install a USB card.

Note
For the fastest speed, buy a USB 2.0 card.

1. Purchase a USB card from a computer or electronics store or from an Internet retailer.

2. Turn off your computer and unplug it from all electrical outlets. This will prevent you from receiving a serious electrical shock and will protect the computer from being damaged.

3. Disconnect all wires and cables from the back of the computer's base unit, and then place the unit on a wooden floor or table. Do not attempt to perform any hands-on computer work while standing or sitting on a carpet or rug. Doing so can generate static electricity that can travel from your body into the computer and damage or destroy your hardware.

4. Remove the computer's cover. For more information, refer to the section "Open Your Computer's Case" in Chapter 12.

5. Locate an empty PCI slot (see Figure 13-3), and then remove the slot's metal or plastic cover by unfastening the screw or plastic arm that holds it in place.

6. Firmly but gently insert the USB card into the empty PCI slot.

7. Secure the USB card by fastening a screw or snapping the plastic arm back into place (see Figure 13-4).

Figure 13-3: Example of an empty PCI slot

Figure 13-4: Securing the PCI card

8. If any wires or cables inside the computer were accidentally disconnected while installing the USB card, reconnect them.

9. Close the case, and then return the base unit to your desk.

10. Reconnect the wires and cables into the back of the base unit, and then plug the computer into an electrical outlet and turn it on.

11. After Windows detects the new USB card, it searches for a "driver" to finish the setup. If the correct driver isn't found, you will need to install it by using the setup CD that came with the USB card.

Add a FireWire Card

FireWire is another type of high-speed connection used by many computer peripherals such as external hard drives and video cameras. (However, FireWire is not used with as many peripherals as USB is.) Similar to USB, FireWire capabilities can be added to a computer by installing a special card.

1. Purchase a FireWire card from a computer or electronics store or from an Internet retailer.

2. Turn off your computer and unplug it from all electrical outlets. This will prevent you from receiving a serious electrical shock and will protect the computer from being damaged.

3. Disconnect all wires and cables from the back of the computer's base unit, and then place the unit on a wooden floor or table. Do not attempt to perform any hands-on computer work while standing or sitting on a carpet or rug. Doing so can generate static electricity that can travel from your body into the computer and damage or destroy your hardware.

4. Remove the computer's cover. For more information, refer to the section "Open Your Computer's Case" in Chapter 12.

5. Locate an empty PCI slot (see Figure 13-5), and then remove the slot's metal or plastic cover by unfastening the screw or plastic arm that holds it in place.

6. Firmly but gently insert the FireWire card into the empty PCI slot.

7. Secure the FireWire card by fastening a screw or by snapping the plastic arm back into place (see Figure 13-6).

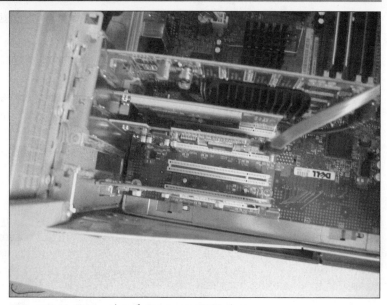

Figure 13-5: Example of an empty PCI slot

Figure 13-6: Securing the PCI card

8. If any wires or cables inside the computer were accidentally disconnected while installing the FireWire card, reconnect them.

9. Close the case, and then return the base unit to your desk.

10. Reconnect the wires and cables into the back of the base unit, and then plug the computer into an electrical outlet and turn it on.

11. After Windows detects the new FireWire card, it searches for a "driver" to finish the setup. If the correct driver isn't found, you need to install it by using the setup CD that came with the FireWire card.

Add a CD or DVD Drive

Have you ever wanted to watch a DVD movie on your computer or make your own custom music CDs? With a modern CD or DVD drive, both activities are possible — and much more. Here are the different types of CD or DVD drives currently available:

- **Read-Only:** These drives can only read information on prerecorded discs. Examples include CD-ROM and DVD-ROM.

- **Recordable or rewritable:** These drives can read data on prerecorded discs and write (or "burn") data onto blank discs. Examples include CD-R, CD-RW, DVD-R, DVD-RW, DVD+R, and DVD+RW. Most of these drives are restricted to using one type of disc. That means "minus R" (-R) drives cannot use "plus R" (+R) discs, and vice versa.

- **Combo drives:** These drives can read and burn data on any type of disc. They are an ideal choice for people who don't want to worry about what type of discs to buy.

To install a CD or DVD drive in your computer, do the following:

1. Purchase a CD or DVD drive from a computer or electronics store or from an Internet retailer.

2. Turn off your computer and unplug it from all electrical outlets. This will prevent you from receiving a serious electrical shock and will protect the computer from being damaged.

3. Disconnect all wires and cables from the back of the computer's base unit, and then place the unit on a wooden floor or table. Do not attempt to perform any hands-on computer work while standing or sitting on a carpet or rug. Doing so can generate static electricity that can travel from your body into the computer and damage or destroy your hardware.

4. Remove the computer's cover. For more information, refer to the section "Open Your Computer's Case" in Chapter 12.

5. On the rear of the new CD or DVD drive is a tiny plastic "jumper" that must be placed onto the small metal pins in a specific way to allow the drive to work side by side with the hard drives or other CD/DVD drives in your system. On the top or rear of most CD or DVD drives is a diagram or picture that shows where to place the jumper to make the drive a "slave." Although many CD or DVD drives are already configured to be slaves, yours may not be. In that case, follow the diagram or picture to make your new drive a slave.

6. Connect a data cable to the new CD or DVD drive. To do so, find the ribbon cable connected to your hard drive, and then use the gray connector in the middle of it to connect to your CD or DVD drive.

7. Connect a power cable to the new CD or DVD drive. Usually all computers have extra power cables tucked away inside their cases.

8. If you want to hear audio from any CDs or DVDs played on your new drive, you may need to connect an audio cable between the drive and the CD-audio input slot on your sound card or motherboard. For more details, refer to the owner's manual or documents that came with your computer.

9. Find an empty mounting bay inside the computer's case, and then slide the new CD or DVD drive into the bay and secure it (usually by screwing the drive to the case).

10. If any wires or cables inside the computer were accidentally disconnected while installing the CD or DVD drive, reconnect them.

11. Close the case, and then return the base unit to your desk.

12. Reconnect the wires and cables into the back of the base unit, and then plug the computer into an electrical outlet and turn it on.

13. Windows should automatically detect the new CD or DVD drive and enable you to use it right away.

Replace Your Floppy Drive

Most people no longer use old-fashioned floppy disks, which is why many new computers don't include floppy drives. However, if you still have old files or programs from many years ago stored on flop-pies, you should consider keeping a floppy drive in your computer. If your drive no longer works — or if you don't have one — you can buy a brand new one for a few dollars and install it yourself.

1. Purchase a floppy drive from a computer or electronics store or from an Internet retailer.

2. Turn off your computer and unplug it from all electrical out-lets. This will prevent you from receiving a serious electrical shock and will protect the computer from being damaged.

3. Disconnect all wires and cables from the back of the com-puter's base unit, and then place the unit on a wooden floor or table. Do not attempt to perform any hands-on computer work while standing or sitting on a carpet or rug. Doing so can generate static electricity that can travel from your body into the computer and damage or destroy your hardware.

4. Remove the computer's cover. For more information, refer to the section "Open Your Computer's Case" in Chapter 12.

5. Disconnect the data cable and power cable from your old floppy drive.

6. Remove the old floppy drive by unscrewing it from its mounting bay. (Newer computers may use plastic clips or other items to secure it.)

7. Connect the data cable and power cable to your new floppy drive.

8. Place the new drive into the empty floppy-drive mounting bay, and then secure it with the screws or plastic clips.

9. If any wires or cables inside the computer were accidentally disconnected while installing the floppy drive, reconnect them.

10. Close the case, and then return the base unit to your desk.

11. Reconnect the wires and cables into the back of the base unit, and then plug the computer into an electrical outlet and turn it on.

12. Windows should automatically detect the new floppy drive and enable you to use it right away.

Add a Dial-Up Modem

If you use a dial-up Internet service, you may be frustrated by unusually slow website connections or downloads that seem to take forever. Before griping to your Internet provider, consider this: The problem may be your modem. If your computer is quite old, it may not be equipped with a 56k modem (which is the fastest speed available over traditional phone lines). Fortunately, it is inexpensive and easy to install a new modem.

1. Purchase a dial-up modem from a computer or electronics store or from an Internet retailer.

2. Turn off your computer and unplug it from all electrical outlets. This will prevent you from receiving a serious electrical shock and will protect the computer from being damaged.

3. Disconnect all wires and cables from the back of the computer's base unit, and then place the unit on a wooden floor or table. Do not attempt to perform any hands-on computer work while standing or sitting on a carpet or rug. Doing so can generate static electricity that can travel from your body into the computer and damage or destroy your hardware.

4. Remove the computer's cover. For more information, refer to the section "Open Your Computer's Case" in Chapter 12.

5. Locate an empty PCI slot (see Figure 13-7), and then remove the slot's metal or plastic cover by unfastening the screw or plastic arm that holds it in place.

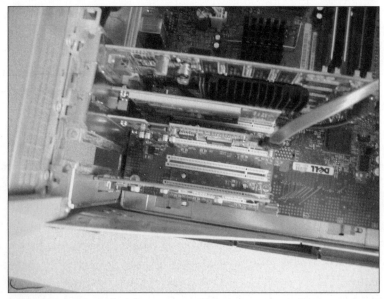

Figure 13-7: Example of an empty PCI slot

6. Firmly but gently insert the modem into the empty PCI slot.

7. Secure the modem by fastening a screw or snapping the plastic arm back into place (see Figure 13-8).

Figure 13-8: Securing the PCI card

8. If any wires or cables inside the computer were accidentally disconnected while installing the modem, reconnect them.

9. Close the case, and then return the base unit to your desk.

10. Reconnect the wires and cables into the back of the base unit, and then plug the computer into an electrical outlet and turn it on.

11. After Windows detects the new modem, it searches for a "driver" to finish the setup. If the correct driver isn't found, you need to install it by using the setup CD that came with the modem.

Note

If you ever cancel your dial-up Internet service and sign up for broadband (high-speed Internet), keep the dial-up modem in your computer. That way, if you ever move to a location that doesn't offer broadband, you can still access the Internet.

Add a Network Card

To connect to a high-speed Internet service such as DSL or cable, your computer must have a wired network card (also called an Ethernet card) or a wireless network card (also called a Wi-Fi card).

1. Purchase an Ethernet or Wi-Fi card from a computer or electronics store or from an Internet retailer.

2. Turn off your computer and unplug it from all electrical outlets. This will prevent you from receiving a serious electrical shock and will protect the computer from being damaged.

3. Disconnect all wires and cables from the back of the computer's base unit, and then place the unit on a wooden floor or table. Do not attempt to perform any hands-on computer work while standing or sitting on a carpet or rug. Doing so can generate static electricity that can travel from your body into the computer and damage or destroy your hardware.

4. Remove the computer's cover. For more information, refer to the section "Open Your Computer's Case" found in Chapter 12.

5. Locate an empty PCI slot (see Figure 13-9), and then remove the slot's metal or plastic cover by unfastening the screw or plastic arm that holds it in place.

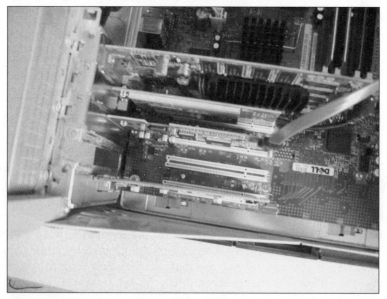

Figure 13-9: Example of an empty PCI slot

6. Firmly but gently insert the network card into the empty PCI slot.

7. Secure the network card by fastening a screw or snapping the plastic arm back into place (see Figure 13-10).

Figure 13-10: Securing the PCI card

8. If any wires or cables inside the computer were accidentally disconnected while installing the network card, reconnect them.

9. Close the case, and then return the base unit to your desk.

10. Reconnect the wires and cables into the back of the base unit, and then plug the computer into an electrical outlet and turn it on.

11. After Windows detects the network card, it searches for a "driver" to finish the setup. If the correct driver isn't found, you need to install it by using the setup CD that came with the network card.

Note

Even if you use a Wi-Fi card, it is a good idea to have an Ethernet card in your computer as a backup.

Replace Your Video Card

A video card is the important piece of hardware that sends images from your computer to your monitor. If the bulk of your computer activities involves the use of programs such as Microsoft Word, Outlook, and Internet Explorer, you don't need a powerful video card. However, if you want to play the newest PC video games that have cutting-edge graphics, you will need to upgrade to a fast video card.

1. Find out what type of video card your computer uses (PCI, AGP, or PCIe) by referring to section "Determine the Video Card's Interface" in Chapter 12.

2. Purchase a new video card from a computer or electronics store or from an Internet retailer.

3. Turn off your computer and unplug it from all electrical outlets. This will prevent you from receiving a serious electrical shock and will protect the computer from being damaged.

4. Disconnect all wires and cables from the back of the computer's base unit, and then place the unit on a wooden floor or table. Do not attempt to perform any hands-on computer work while standing or sitting on a carpet or rug. Doing so can generate static electricity that can travel from your body into the computer and damage or destroy your hardware.

5. Remove the computer's cover. For more information, refer to the section "Open Your Computer's Case" in Chapter 12.

6. Based on the type of interface used by your new video card, locate an empty PCI slot, an empty AGP slot, or an empty PCIe slot. Remove the slot's metal or plastic cover by unfastening the screw or plastic arm that holds it in place.

7. Firmly but gently insert the video card into the appropriate slot.

8. Secure the video card by fastening a screw or snapping the plastic arm back into place (see Figure 13-11).

9. If any wires or cables inside the computer were accidentally disconnected while installing the video card, reconnect them.

10. Close the case, and then return the base unit to your desk.

Figure 13-11: Securing the PCI card

11. Reconnect the wires and cables into the back of the base unit, and then plug the computer into an electrical outlet and turn it on.

12. After Windows detects the new video card, it searches for a "driver" to finish the setup. Do not use the standard, default drivers that Windows installs. The only way to enjoy the powerful features of your new video card is to install the special drivers and software located on the setup CD that came with it.

Replace Your Sound Card

If you enjoy playing video games or watching DVD movies on your computer, you should consider upgrading your sound card to one that has enhanced features such as Dolby Digital 5.1 or 7.1 surround sound.

1. Purchase a new sound card from a computer or electronics store or from an Internet retailer.

2. Turn off your computer and unplug it from all electrical outlets. This will prevent you from receiving a serious electrical
shock and will protect the computer from being damaged.

3. Disconnect all wires and cables from the back of the computer's base unit, and then place the unit on a wooden floor
or table. Do not attempt to perform any hands-on computer
work while standing or sitting on a carpet or rug. Doing so
can generate static electricity that can travel from your body
into the computer and damage or destroy your hardware.

4. Remove the computer's cover. For more information, refer
to the section "Open Your Computer's Case" found in
Chapter 12.

5. Locate an empty PCI slot (see Figure 13-12), and then
remove the slot's metal or plastic cover by unfastening the
screw or plastic arm that holds it in place.

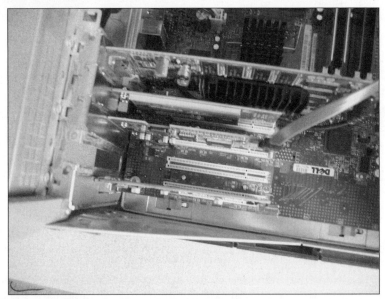

Figure 13-12: Example of an empty PCI slot

6. Firmly but gently insert the sound card into the empty PCI
slot.

7. Secure the sound card by fastening a screw or snapping the
plastic arm back into place (see Figure 13-13).

Figure 13-13: Securing the PCI card

8. If any wires or cables inside the computer were accidentally disconnected while installing the sound card, reconnect them.

9. Close the case, and then return the base unit to your desk.

10. Reconnect the wires and cables into the back of the base unit, and then plug the computer into an electrical outlet and turn it on.

11. After Windows detects the new sound card, it searches for a "driver" to finish the setup. Do not use the standard, default drivers that Windows installs. The only way to enjoy the powerful features of your new sound card is to install the special drivers and software located on the setup CD that came with it.

14

INSTALLING PERIPHERALS

Half the fun of using a computer comes from its accessories (usually referred to as "peripherals") such as printers, scanners, and digital cameras. In case you decided to upgrade your PC after using CA's PC Pitstop Optimize, this chapter is here to explain how to install and set up common peripherals and provides fixes for problems you might run into.

Use Newer Gadgets on Older PCs

To make a modern peripheral work on an outdated version of Windows such as 98 or ME, you need to install small pieces of software called "drivers" that tell Windows how to interact with the device. Usually all peripherals come with an installation CD-ROM containing the proper drivers, but if you have lost this CD or never received it (which often happens when you buy a used peripheral from a place like eBay), you will need to download the drivers.

1. Open your web browser and visit the manufacturer's website.

2. Find the section of the site either labeled Support or Downloads, and search for information about drivers.

3. You probably will need to know the make and model of your product (so you may need to look on its exterior for that information).

4. Find the drivers that are designed to work with your version of Windows. Usually, the downloads will come in the form of an executable program. If so, download the executable to a folder on your computer that you can easily locate.

5. Double-click the executable to begin the installation of the drivers.

6. Try connecting your product again.

Add a Surge Protector

Did you know it is dangerous to plug your computer or other gadgets directly into an electrical outlet? A thunderstorm or power surge can send intense bursts of electricity racing through the power lines in your home or office. These bursts can travel into your computer and fry it — or even worse, they can cause your computer to catch fire, which in turn could ignite the rest of your building. To prevent this from happening, use a device known as a surge protector.

Note

Not all surge protectors provide the same protection. Generally, the more expensive one is, the better protection it offers.

1. Properly shut down your PC and other equipment.

2. Unplug your PC and related equipment from the power strip or electrical outlet to which they are currently connected.

3. Plug your new surge protector into an available electrical outlet.

4. Plug your PC and other equipment into the outlets on the surge protector (see Figure 14-1).

5. Most surge protectors have an On/Off switch. Make sure this switch is set to the On position (which usually causes a light to turn on).

6. Turn on your computer and peripherals and use them as you normally would.

Figure 14-1: Plugging into a surge protector

Add a Battery Backup

A battery backup (also known as an uninterruptible power supply) is a device that not only serves as a surge protector, but also has a large battery that provides emergency electricity during a power outage or brown-out. Originally, battery backups were designed only to provide a few minutes of power—just enough to save your open computer files and safely shut down your computer—but modern ones can often supply an hour or more.

1. Properly shut down your PC and other equipment.

2. Unplug your PC and related equipment from the power strip or electrical outlet to which they are currently connected.

3. Plug your new battery backup into an available electrical outlet.

4. Plug your PC and other equipment into the battery backup's outlets. Keep in mind that most battery backups have only a few outlets that connect to the backup system, while the others are just regular or surge-protected outlets.

5. Nearly every battery backup has an On/Off switch. Make sure this switch is set to the On position (which usually causes a light to turn on).

Add a USB Hub

If you have a lot of USB devices to connect to your computer but not enough USB ports, you can add more by installing a USB hub. Basically a hub is a small box that plugs into a single USB port on your computer. On the hub are usually between two and six USB ports. Instead of reaching around the back of your computer to plug in a USB device such as a digital camera, you can simply plug that device directly into the hub. Here's how to install a hub:

Note

If your computer supports high-speed USB 2.0 devices, be sure to buy a hub that also handles USB 2.0.

1. Most USB hubs have a USB cable built into them. If that is the case with your hub, connect the cable to an available USB port on your computer. If your hub has a detachable USB cable, plug one end into the hub and the other end into an available USB port on your computer.

2. Most USB hubs do not have a separate power cord, because they receive electricity through the USB cable. However, if your hub has a separate power cord, connect the appropriate end into the hub and the other end into an electrical outlet.

3. Plug your USB devices into the hub (see Figure 14-2).

Figure 14-2: Example of a USB hub

Replace Your Speakers

If you enjoy using your computer to play video games or watch DVD movies, you should consider replacing your old, simple speakers with a state-of-the-art set. Most modern computer speakers come with a subwoofer to provide booming bass, and you can even buy an entire surround-sound system designed to work perfectly with your computer. To install new speakers, follow these steps:

1. Shut down your PC.

2. If your sound system has a subwoofer, do the following:

    a. Plug your speakers into the subwoofer.

    b. Plug the subwoofer into the audio-output connector on your computer.

    c. Connect one end of the power cord into the subwoofer and the other end into an electrical outlet.

3. If your sound system does not have a subwoofer, do the following:

    a. Plug one of the speakers into the main speaker.

    b. Plug the main speaker into the audio-output connector on your computer.

    c. Connect one end of the power cord into the main speaker and the other end into an electrical outlet.

Note

If you are buying a surround-sound system for your computer, make sure it is compatible with Dolby Digital 5.1 or 7.1.

Replace Your Monitor

If your computer monitor is too small or doesn't produce a bright, sharp picture anymore, the best thing to do is replace it.

1. Shut down your computer and monitor.

2. Disconnect the monitor's video cable from the computer, and then unplug the monitor's power cable from the electrical outlet.

3. Move your old monitor out of the way, and then move the
new one into place.

4. Connect your new monitor's video cable to your computer's video card.

5. Connect one end of the power cord to the new monitor,
and then plug the other end into an electrical outlet.

6. Turn on your computer and your new monitor.

Clean Your Mouse

If you are using an old-fashioned computer mouse—the kind with a
movable ball—you might notice that sometimes the mouse's on-
screen cursor doesn't immediately respond to the movements of your
hand. Usually the cause is dirt, hair, or other debris that has accu-
mulated inside the mouse (see Figure 14-3). Fortunately, there is an
easy solution: Clean your mouse.

1. Shut down your computer.

2. Unplug the mouse from the back of your computer.

3. Remove the cover on the bottom of the mouse. Usually this
is done by pushing down and turning the cover in the
direction indicated by the arrows etched on it.

4. When the cover opens, you will see a small rubber ball. Set
the ball aside, but be careful not to lose it.

5. You will see three rollers inside the mouse. Use the tip of a
pen, tweezers, or your fingernails to remove the debris from
the rollers.

6. Clean your mouse ball with a warm, damp cloth. Make
sure the ball is dry before proceeding to the next step.

7. Insert the ball into the mouse (see Figure 14-4), and then
reattach the cover.

8. Plug the mouse back into your computer, and then turn on
your computer.

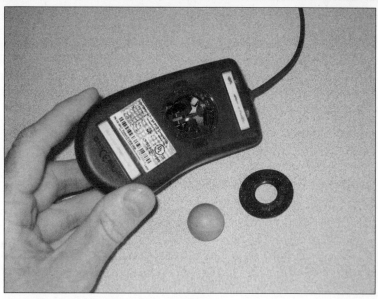

Figure 14-3: Unassembled mouse

Figure 14-4: Assembling a mouse

Replace Your Mouse

Instead of using an old-fashioned mouse that needs to be cleaned every few months, consider replacing it with an optical mouse that doesn't use a ball. Instead, it uses a laser beam, which means the movements of your hand will be more accurately recognized and displayed on the screen. Here's how to install a new mouse:

Note

Most modern mice use USB connectors. If your computer doesn't have any USB ports, you will need to use a "PS/2 to USB" adapter.

1. If your new mouse is designed to use a USB interface, you can simply plug it into your computer while the computer is running. If your new mouse does not use USB, you must turn off your computer before connecting the mouse.

2. Unplug your current mouse.

3. Plug your new mouse into your computer's PS/2 or USB port.

4. Turn on your computer (if necessary) and start using your new mouse.

5. If your mouse came with a CD-ROM containing software that will enhance its features and performance, install that software.

Replace Your Keyboard

The keyboards that come with most computers tend to be very simple, lacking advanced features. If you want to replace your old keyboard with one that has multimedia buttons, shortcut keys, and many other enhancements, do the following:

Note

Most modern keyboards use USB connectors. If your computer doesn't have any USB ports, you will need to use a "PS/2 to USB" adapter.

1. If your new keyboard is designed to use a USB interface, you can simply plug it into your computer while the computer is running. If your new keyboard does not use USB, you must turn off your computer before connecting the keyboard.

2. Unplug your current keyboard.

3. Plug your new keyboard into your computer's PS/2 or USB port (see Figure 14-5).

Figure 14-5: Plugging in the keyboard

4. Turn on your computer (if necessary) and start using your new keyboard.

5. If your new keyboard has special features such as program-mable buttons or a built-in video game controller, you will probably need to install special software by using the CD-ROM that came with the keyboard.

Connect a Printer

Almost all printers available today use USB interfaces. To connect a USB printer to your computer, follow these steps:

1. Most printers come with a USB cable (see Figure 14-6). Connect one end of the cable to the USB port on the printer, and then connect the other end of the cable to a USB port on your computer.

2. If the printer's power cord is not permanently attached, plug one end of it into the printer and plug the other end into an electrical outlet.

Figure 14-6: Connecting a printer

3. Windows should detect the new printer and search for "drivers" to complete the installation. If Windows cannot find them, you will have to install the proper drivers by using the installation CD that came with the printer or by downloading them from the manufacturer's website.

4. Use the CD that came with your printer to install the special software that will enable the printer to function properly.

Configure Printer Preferences

After you have installed a printer, you should configure its settings. Doing so can make your ink cartridges last longer, speed up printing time, and produce nicer-looking • prints.

For Windows XP Home/Pro and Windows 2000:

1. Click the Start button in the lower-left corner of Windows.

2. Click the Control Panel. If you don't see this option, your Start menu is in classic mode. In that case, click Settings, and then select the Control Panel.

3. If the Control Panel is in category view, click the Printers and Other Hardware category, and then click the Printers and Faxes icon. If the Control Panel is in classic view, simply double-click the Printers and Faxes icon.

4. Right-click the printer you want to configure.

5. Click Printer Preferences.

6. Printer preferences differ based on the computer and printer you are using, so you need to explore the available settings by clicking the various tabs and selecting or deselecting the numerous options. For example, you can change the printer quality (see Figure 14-7), the print color, the orientation (either "landscape" or "portrait" as shown in Figure 14-8), and the print order (front to back or back to front).

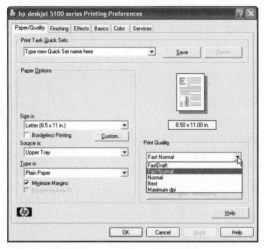

Figure 14-7: Print Quality options

Figure 14-8: Print Orientation options

For Windows 98 and ME:

1. Click the Start button in the lower-left corner of Windows.

2. Click Settings.

3. Click Printers.

4. Right-click the printer you want to configure.

5. Click Printer Preferences.

6. Printer preferences differ based on the computer and printer you are using, so you need to explore the available settings by clicking the various tabs and selecting or deselecting the numerous options. For example, you can change the print quality (see Figure 14-9), the print color, the orientation (either "landscape" or "portrait" as shown in Figure 14-10), and the print order (front to back or back to front).

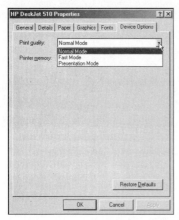

Figure 14-9: Print Quality options

Figure 14-10: Print Orientation options

Note

To conserve ink and print documents faster, use a low-quality setting when printing average, unimportant documents. When you need to print special documents and official reports for work or school, return the print quality to a higher level.

Connect a Digital Camera

One of the best things about using a digital camera is the ease with which you can connect it to your computer, transfer your photos to your hard drive, and then email them to your friends and family— without having to get them processed by a photo lab. To connect a digital camera to your PC, follow these steps:

1. Most digital cameras come with a USB cable. Connect one end of the cable to the USB port on the digital camera, and then connect the other end of the cable to a USB port on your computer.

2. If you are using Windows XP, you will likely see a window that tells you a device has been connected and asks what program you would like to launch. To use this Windows utility to view and copy your pictures to your PC, select Microsoft Scanner and Camera Wizard, and then click OK (see Figure 14-11).

Figure 14-11: Camera Alert window

3. If you are using Windows 98, the Found New Hardware Wizard will likely pop up and ask you to install the drivers from the setup CD. Also, you will need to install the software included on that same CD in order to transfer photos to and from the camera.

Connect a Camcorder

If you own a digital camcorder that you use to make home movies, it probably has a USB or FireWire connector. If so, you can hook up the camcorder to your computer, transfer the video to your hard drive, and edit it. To connect a camcorder to your PC, follow these steps:

1. Most digital camcorders come with a USB or FireWire cable. Connect one end of the cable to the USB or FireWire port on the camcorder, and then connect the other end of the cable to a USB or FireWire port on your computer.

2. Windows should detect the new camcorder and search for "drivers" to complete the installation. If Windows cannot find them, you will have to install the proper drivers by using the installation CD that came with the camcorder or by downloading them from the manufacturer's website.

3. Use the CD that came with the camcorder to install a special video-editing program, which will enable you to transfer video clips to and from your computer and edit those clips.

Connect a Video Game Controller

To play video games on your computer, you need to connect a game controller such as a joystick, gamepad, or steering wheel.

Note
These steps apply only to USB video game controllers.

1. Connect your controller to a USB port on your computer.

2. Windows should detect the new controller and search for "drivers" to complete the installation. If Windows cannot find them, you will have to install the proper drivers by using the installation CD that came with the controller or by downloading them from the manufacturer's website.

3. After installation, configure and customize your controller by doing the following:

    a. Click the Start button in the lower-left corner of Windows.

    b. Click the Control Panel. (If you don't see this option, your Start menu is in classic mode. In that case, click Settings, and then select the Control Panel.)

   c. If the Control Panel is in category view, click the Printers and Other Hardware category, and then click the Game Controllers icon. If the Control Panel is in classic view, simply double-click the Game Controllers icon.

   d. A window opens. In it, click the name of your controller, and then click the Properties button.

Connect a Scanner

If you have a large collection of family photos you want to preserve by digitizing them into your computer, you will need to install a scanner.

For USB and FireWire Scanners:

1. Most scanners come with a USB or FireWire cable. Connect one end of the cable to the USB or FireWire port on the scanner, and then connect the other end of the cable to a USB or FireWire port on your computer.

2. Most new scanners have their scanning heads locked to prevent them from being damaged. To unlock the scanning head, look for a knob or lever located near the scanner's power cord or on/off switch.

3. Connect the power cord to the scanner, and then plug the other end into an electrical outlet.

4. Windows should detect the new scanner and search for "drivers" to complete the installation. If Windows cannot find them, you will have to install the proper drivers by using the installation CD that came with the scanner or by downloading them from the manufacturer's website.

For Parallel-Port Scanners:

1. Shut down your computer before connecting the scanner.

2. Disconnect any devices that are currently connected to your computer's parallel port.

3. Connect one end of the parallel-port cable (which should have been included with your scanner) to the parallel port on the scanner, and then connect the other end to the parallel port on your computer.

4. If you disconnected a printer from the computer's parallel port, connect it to the printer port on the scanner.

5. Most new scanners have their scanning heads locked to prevent them from being damaged. To unlock the scanning head, look for a knob or lever located near the scanner's power cord or on/off switch.

6. Connect the power cord to the scanner, and then plug the other end into an electrical outlet.

7. Turn on your computer.

8. Windows should detect the new scanner and search for "drivers" to complete the installation. If Windows cannot find them, you will have to install the proper drivers by using the installation CD that came with the scanner or by downloading them from the manufacturer's website.

15

TROUBLESHOOTING COMPUTERS

L et's face it: Sometimes computers can be so frustrating that they make you want to abandon them forever and switch to an old-fashioned, reliable typewriter. If after using CA's PC Pitstop Optimize you still have problems with your PC, then scan through this chapter to learn how to troubleshoot and solve common PC problems.

Computer Randomly Crashes or Displays Blue Screen

If you have used Windows for several years, you have probably experienced occasional freezes, crashes, or the error messages jokingly referred to as "blue screens of death" (see Figure 15-1). If shutting down and restarting your computer doesn't solve these problems, you might benefit from the fixes in the following categories.

Software Troubles

1. If you recently installed a new program, try uninstalling it. For more information, see the section "Software Installation Goes Horribly Wrong" later in this chapter.

2. If uninstalling the software solves your problem, contact its manufacturer for information on how to install the program properly so it won't conflict with Windows or with your other software.

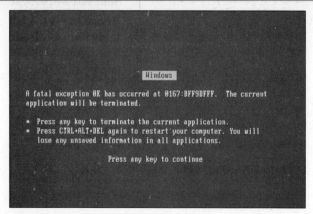

Figure 15-1: Example of a blue screen

Overheated Computer

1. Download software to analyze the temperature inside your computer. If you find the temperature in your computer to be near the upper limit, which is generally 120 degrees Fahrenheit, overheating is probably causing your problems.

2. Move your computer's base unit so that it is at least 6 to 12 inches away from all walls, desks, or anything else that might prevent air from flowing into your PC through its fans and exhaust ports.

3. Listen for the sound of your computer's internal cooling fans. If you don't hear them, they may have malfunctioned. In that case, replace them.

Malfunctioning USB Hub

1. If you have a USB hub, disconnect it for a few hours to see if it is the source of your troubles.

2. If removing the hub does not correct your problems, go ahead and reconnect it.

If you have tried these fixes and your PC still has problems, it is possible that it might have a software conflict, faulty memory, or a malfunctioning hard drive. In that case, contact a computer professional.

Nothing Happens When the Computer Is Turned On

If you attempt to start your computer but nothing happens — no lights, no fan noise, no sounds, nothing — follow these steps:

1. Make sure your computer and your monitor are plugged into a power strip or an electrical outlet.

2. If you are using a power strip, check to see if it is actually plugged into an electrical outlet and is turned on. Most surge protectors have an On/Off switch. Make sure this switch is set to the On position (which usually causes a light to turn on).

3. Find out if the electricity in your home or office has malfunctioned:

   a. See whether the lights in your room are working.

   b. Plug a light into your computer's power strip to see if that strip is working properly. It is possible that the power strip has malfunctioned.

4. If you are certain that both your computer and monitor are receiving electrical power, it is possible that the power supply or another piece of hardware inside your computer has died. In that case, call a computer professional.

Computer Takes a Long Time to Power Up

Having a computer that is slow to start up doesn't necessarily mean there is something wrong with it. The slowness can be caused by important programs that often take a while to load (such as anti-virus software) or by having too many programs on your computer. Your first remedy is to remove any software you no longer use (such as old video games). If that doesn't work, try adding more RAM to your computer by following the section "Add More System Memory (RAM)" in Chapter 13. If the slowness continues, try reducing the amount of programs that load when Windows starts. Here's how:

1. Click the Start button in the lower-left corner of Windows.

2. Click Run.

3. A window opens. Type **msconfig** in the blank, and then click OK or press the Enter key on your keyboard.

4. A window named System Configuration Utility opens. Click the Startup tab on the far right.

5. In the left column (Startup Item) is a list of programs with checkmarks next to them (see Figure 15-2). A checkmark indicates that the program is scheduled to launch each time Windows starts. To prevent a program from loading at startup, remove the checkmark from its box. Here are guidelines about which programs to allow or to disable:

- Disable nonessential multimedia programs such as qttask (which is part of the QuickTime software), realsched (which is part of the RealPlayer software), or Adobe Reader.

- Allow common processes for Windows and Microsoft Office.

- Allow programs related to your anti-virus software, anti-spyware software, or firewall.

- Allow programs related to your printer. For example, if you have an Epson printer, allow the startup program named Epson Status Monitor.

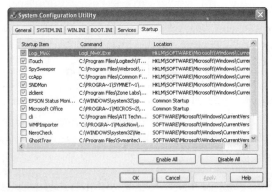

Figure 15-2: System Configuration Utility

6. When you have finished tweaking the System Configuration Utility, click Apply.

7. Click OK.

8. A message alerts you that you must restart your computer for the changes to take effect. Click the Restart button. Your computer automatically shuts down and reboots.

9. When you return to Windows, a message alerts you that you have just used the System Configuration Utility to change the way Windows starts. Put a checkmark in the Don't Show This Message or Launch the System Configuration Utility When Windows Starts box.

10. Click OK.

Note

You may discover an application or process isn't working properly after you have made changes to the startup items, and you may want to undo the changes. You can go back to the System Configuration utility, re-check the checkboxes you unchecked, and see if that solves your problem.

Computer Continuously Accesses the Hard Drive

Does the hard drive in your computer sound like it is running non-stop? Does the small light on the front of your computer constantly flash, indicating that the hard drive is always being used? If so, your hard drive may be overworked because you don't have enough system memory (RAM). Here's what to do:

1. Restart your computer.

2. Check how much RAM your computer has. For more information, refer to the section "Determine Your Amount of System Memory (RAM)" in Chapter 12.

3. Add more memory, preferably twice as much as your current amount. For more information on doing this, refer to the section "Add More System Memory (RAM)" in Chapter 13.

Laptop Battery Life Is Too Short

Laptop computers are quite convenient — assuming they have power. If you can't plug a laptop into an electrical outlet, it has to rely on batteries. Most laptops run only two to three hours on a fully charged battery. To extend the life of your laptop's battery, do the following:

1. Lower the brightness of your screen.

2. Disable your wireless card. To do so, double-click the wireless icon in the lower-right corner of Windows, and then click Disable (see Figure 15-3).

Figure 15-3: Disabling a wireless network card

3. To reduce the battery's usage and extends its life, configure the power options in Windows.

For Windows XP and Windows 2000:

    a. Click the Start button in the lower-left corner of Windows.

    b. Click Control Panel. If you don't see this option, your Start menu is in classic mode. In that case, click Settings and then select the Control Panel.

    c. If the Control Panel is in category view, click the Performance and Maintenance category and then click the Power Options icon. If the Control Panel is in classic view, simply double-click the Power Options icon.

    d. Select an appropriate Power Scheme (see Figure 15-4).

    e. Click OK.

Figure 15-4: Selecting a power option

For Windows 98 and Windows ME:

    a. Click the Start button in the lower-left corner of Windows.

    b. Click the Control Panel.

    c. Double-click Power Management.

    d. Select an appropriate Power Scheme.

    e. Click OK.

4. If your battery continues to last for less than one hour, replace it.

Monitor Has Poor Image Quality

Poor image quality on your computer's monitor can be annoying in more ways than one. Not only does it make fine details in photos or videos difficult to see, but it also causes eye strain. If the images on your monitor look grainy or distorted, try the following:

1. Increase the resolution of your monitor:

    a. Right-click in the empty space on your desktop.

    b. Select Properties.

    c. A window opens. Select the Settings tab.

    d. Move the Screen Resolution slider bar to a higher resolution. If your current resolution is 640 × 480 pixels, move it to 800 × 600 pixels. If your current resolution is 800 × 600 pixels, move it to 1,024 × 768 pixels (see Figure 15-5).

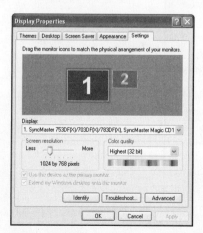

Figure 15-5: Choosing a screen resolution

2. Unplug the monitor from your computer and look for bent or missing pins on the end of the monitor's video cable. If some are bent, try straightening them. If some are missing, you will need to replace the cable.

3. If the images on your monitor are poor or grainy only when you use a specific program such as a video game, you may need to upgrade your video card to a newer model that can handle advanced graphics. For more information, refer to the section "Replace Your Video Card" in Chapter 13.

Screen Flickers

If your computer's monitor appears to constantly flicker or blink, its "refresh rate" is probably too low. Rather than suffer eye strain by continuing to use your PC under those conditions, you should increase the refresh rate.

For Windows XP Home/Pro and Windows 2000:

1. Right-click in the empty space on your desktop.

2. Select Properties.

3. A window opens. Click the Settings tab.

4. Click the Advanced button.

5. Click the Monitor tab.

6. Choose a higher refresh rate (if available). Generally you want 75 Hertz or higher (see Figure 15-6).

Figure 15-6: Choosing a refresh rate

7. Click OK.

8. If this doesn't fix the problem, you may need to replace the monitor.

For Windows 98 and Windows ME:

1. Right-click in the empty space on your desktop.

2. Select Properties.

3. A window opens. Click the Settings tab.

4. Click the Advanced button.

5. Click the Adapter tab.

6. Choose a higher refresh rate (if available). Generally, you want 75 Hertz or higher.

7. Click OK.

8. If this doesn't fix the problem, you may need to replace the monitor.

Invalid System Disk While Booting

If, after turning on your computer, you see a message that says you have an invalid system disk or that you need to remove a disk, you can easily solve this problem:

1. Eject the floppy disk from your floppy drive.

2. Press any key on your keyboard to restart your computer.

Software Installation Goes Horribly Wrong

Once in a while, installing a new program can wreak havoc with your entire computer, causing it to freeze, crash, or not operate normally. If so, do the following:

1. Uninstall the software:

For Windows XP Home/Pro and Windows 2000:

   a. Click the Start button in the lower-left corner of Windows.

   b. Click the Control Panel. If you don't see this option, your Start menu is in classic mode. In that case, click Settings, and then select the Control Panel.

   c. Double-click the Add or Remove Programs icon.

   d. Select the software and click the Remove or
Change/Remove button (see Figure 15-7).

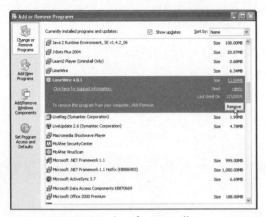

Figure 15-7: Example of uninstalling a program

For Windows 98 and Windows ME:

   a. Click the Start button in the lower-left corner of Windows.

   b. Click Settings.

   c. Click the Control Panel.

   d. Double-click the Add or Remove Programs icon.

   e. Select the software you want to remove, and then click
the Add/Remove button (see Figure 15-8).

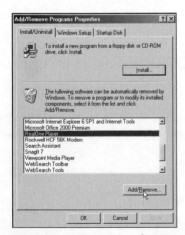

Figure 15-8: Example of uninstalling a program

2. Shut down your computer and restart it.

3. If your computer still has problems after uninstalling the software, you can use a last-ditch fix called System Restore. In a sense, System Restore sends your computer back in time to a day when it was working properly. Here's how to use it:

    a. Click the Start button in the lower-left corner of Windows.

    b. Click All Programs.

    c. Select Accessories.

    d. Select System Tools.

    e. Click the words System Restore.

    f. The System Restore window opens. Click the Restore My Computer to an Earlier Time button (see Figure 15-9).

Figure 15-9: System Restore window

    g. Click the Next button, located near the lower-right corner of this window.

    h. A calendar appears. In it, click a day when your computer was working properly. For example, if your PC had problems after installing Microsoft Works, choose that specific restore point (see Figure 15-10).

    i. Click Next.

    j. To confirm your choice, click Next again.

    k. The System Restore process begins. Moments later, your computer automatically restarts itself. When it boots up, follow the on-screen instructions.

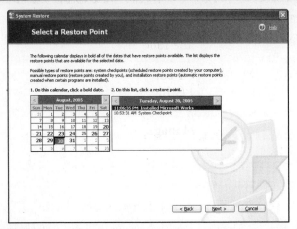

Figure 15-10: Selecting a restore point

New Hardware Doesn't Work

If a new piece of hardware you just connected to your computer doesn't work properly—or not at all—follow these fixes:

1. Make sure you properly followed the hardware's instructions word for word (and make sure you followed the directions that apply to your particular version of Windows).

2. Check the hardware to ensure that it is hooked up correctly and has a secure connection. For example, if you installed a PCI card, make sure it was properly snapped into place and is not loose. Or, if you installed a printer, make sure its connection to the computer is tight and secure.

3. Update Windows with the latest patches and drivers by visiting http://windowsupdate.microsoft.com (don't put a www in front of this Web address).

4. Try uninstalling and then reinstalling the hardware.

5. If the hardware still doesn't work properly, check its documentation or contact its manufacturer by visiting its website or calling its customer support line.

Computer or Software Doesn't Respond

One minute your computer is working fine. The next minute, everything freezes. Windows, your software, and your mouse don't respond to your commands. Sound familiar? If you are a regular user of Windows, this scenario has probably happened to you more than once. The next time it does, try the following:

1. Wait a minute because your computer may just be experiencing a temporary freeze (which can happen if you try to open or run several programs at once).

2. Open the Windows Task Manager by simultaneously pressing the Ctrl, Alt, and Delete keys on your keyboard. If 30 seconds have elapsed and the Task Manager has not opened, proceed to Step 5.

3. When the Task Manager opens, click the Applications tab (see Figure 15-11).

Figure 15-11: Task Manager Applications tab

4. If the Task Manager indicates that a particular task or program is not responding, click its name, and then click the End Task button (see Figure 15-12). If a window pops up and asks whether you want to end the task or program, click the End Task button again.

5. If the troubled task or program continues to be unresponsive — or if your computer as a whole is experiencing problems — save any open documents (if you can), and then turn off your computer by pushing or holding down the power button on the front of your computer. Next, restart the computer.

Figure 15-12: Ending a task

Keyboard Doesn't Respond

If your keyboard suddenly stops working, it might be unplugged or damaged. Here's what to do:

1. Make sure your keyboard is connected to your computer. If not, plug it back in and restart the computer.

2. If your keyboard is connected, slightly wiggle the connector and make sure it fits snugly into the port. Next, restart the computer.

3. If your keyboard uses a PS/2 connector, it is possible that the connector has been damaged or has worn out. Look for bent or missing pins on the end of the connector. If some are bent, try straightening them. If some are missing, you will need to replace the keyboard.

Video Game Doesn't Work Correctly

A common problem experienced by PC video game users is slow or sputtering graphics. If you experience similar issues, here are some tips:

1. Refer to Chapter 12 for information on analyzing your PC. After you know what type of hardware and software your PC has, you can compare it to the system requirements listed on the game's package.

2. If your PC is not compatible with the game's system requirements, you might be able to upgrade some of your hardware

components. For more information on upgrading a PC, refer to Chapter 13.

3. If your PC meets the system requirements, refer to the owner's manual or documentation that came with the video game to see if it provides tips on troubleshooting problems. If the manual doesn't list any tips or if you don't have a manual, contact the game's manufacturer by visiting its website or calling the customer support number.

No Sound

Have your computer's speakers suddenly gone silent? Then one of these fixes should do the trick:

1. If you have external speakers, make sure they have been plugged into an electrical outlet and have been turned on (usually a light will illuminate to indicate that the speakers are powered up).

2. Check to see if the sound on your computer has been turned down or muted. Double-click the sound icon located in the lower-right corner of Windows. If this icon is not available, do the following:

   a. Click the Start button in the lower-left corner of Windows.

   b. Click Programs (or All Programs).

   c. Click Accessories.

   d. Click Entertainment (or Multimedia).

   e. Click Volume Control.

Look for any controls that have been muted or turned down, especially the main volume control (see Figure 15-13). If you can't see all of the controls, click the Options drop-down menu, and then select Properties. Make sure that all of the volume controls are checked; then click OK (see Figure 15-14).

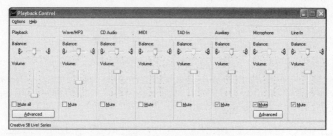

Figure 15-13: Volume Control options

Figure 15-14: Volume controls

3. If you have external speakers, make sure their audio wires or cables are connected properly.

4. If the sound still doesn't work, your sound card or speakers might have to be replaced.

Determine Whether a Program or Game Will Run on Your Computer

Before buying new hardware or software, make sure they will work properly on your computer by following this advice:

1. Refer to Chapter 12 for information on analyzing your PC. After you know what type of hardware and software your PC has, you can compare it to the system requirements listed on the package of the game or program you want to install.

2. If your PC is not compatible with the program's system requirements, you might be able to upgrade some of your hardware components. For more information on upgrading a PC, refer to Chapter 13.

16

BUYING A NEW PC

I f after using CA's PC Pitstop Optimize and attempting troubleshooting you still have problems with your PC, it may be best to purchase a new PC. This chapter steps you through the process to make buying a new PC as painless as possible.

Buying a computer is a lot like buying a car. Both require you to research the numerous makes and models available and carefully select the features—and price tag—that are right for you. Should you go with the humble, no-frills model? What about the turbocharged top-of-the-line model with all the bells and whistles? Is it worth getting an extended warranty? Questions like these can feel overwhelming (and unending). Fortunately, you are not alone in this process. Consider this chapter to be your digital chauffeur, here to help you bypass the traffic jams of overcrowded computer stores and arrive safely at a final decision.

If you already own a computer but are considering replacing it, the first thing you should ask yourself is "Do I really need a new one?" As discussed in Chapter 13, upgrading the broken or outdated parts on a computer is a great way to save time and money and to get the most out of your investment. However, it is true that some PCs are so old or have so many problems that it is easier (and sometimes cheaper) to replace them with new ones.

Here are the most common reasons for buying a new computer:

- **Meeting the demands of modern software:** Many modern programs such as video games or photo/video-editing software need a fast, powerful computer in order to run properly.

- **Eliminating high-tech headaches:** Some computers are so old or have so many problems that it is simpler to get rid of them and start over with a fresh, new system.

- **Upgrading can be difficult:** Because so many people today lead busy lives, they can't afford to spend time learning how to take apart and upgrade a computer.

- **Having the latest and greatest:** Sometimes it can be fun to have the newest cutting-edge equipment and gadgets to play with.

Pick the Perfect PC

If you have carefully considered the great debate about upgrading versus. buying and have decided that a new PC is the best choice for you, your next course of action is to pick the type of computer you need, select a style (desktop or laptop), and consider which additional features you want.

Computer Types

The most important factor to consider when buying a new computer is the activities you anticipate doing on it. How the computer will be used and the number of people using it will determine how many problems it develops, its condition one year from now, its overall lifespan, and more. Here are the four common types of computers. Choose the one that most accurately describes your needs:

- **Light general use:** Used by one to three people for a few hours each day. Activities include typing documents, sending and receiving email, browsing the Internet, and playing older video games that do not have cutting-edge graphics.

- **Heavy general use:** Used by more than three people or used for many hours each day. Activities include typing documents, sending and receiving email, browsing the Internet, and playing video games that have medium-level graphics.

- **Gaming:** Performs all of the activities of a heavy general-use computer and users play video games that have demanding, cutting-edge graphics.

- **High performance:** Meets all the criteria for a gaming computer plus has extra top-of-the-line hardware to handle demanding activities such as using video-editing programs or other heavy-duty, high-performance software.

Note
Spend time thinking about how much your new computer might be used on a daily basis. That information will help you select the appropriate type of computer and get the most out of your investment. For example, if you anticipate using your PC for the majority of each day to do simple, routine tasks such as typing documents, browsing the Internet, and checking email, you should consider buying a heavy general-use computer.

Desktop versus Laptop

After deciding what type of computer suits your needs, you must choose its style: desktop or laptop.

Desktop

As shown in Figure 16-1, a desktop PC is the standard style of computer used in most homes and offices. Here are the advantages and disadvantages of buying a desktop:

- **Low cost:** Most desktop PCs cost under $1,000, and some can be purchased for as little as $300.

- **Versatile:** Can be used for all types of activities, including light general use, heavy general use, gaming, and high performance.

- **Upgradeable:** Probably the best thing about desktop PCs is their ability to be customized and upgraded. If a part breaks down, it can be easily replaced. If you want to add extra hardware to play cutting-edge video games or perform other demanding tasks, that too can be easily done.

- **Stationary:** Unlike a laptop computer, a desktop PC has to remain in one location at all times.

Figure 16-1: Typical desktop PC Laptop

As shown in Figure 16-2, a laptop (also called a notebook computer) is a small, portable computer that is becoming increasingly popular in our on-the-go world. Also, many educational institutions such as high schools and colleges are beginning to require their students to use laptops in the classroom. Here are the advantages and disadvantages of buying a laptop:

- **Mobile:** The freedom to take their computer wherever they go is the number-one reason most laptop users give when explaining why they bought one. However, the downside is that if the laptop is accidentally left behind in a cab, train, or subway, or if it is stolen, all of your computer files will be lost forever (and potentially used by a criminal to commit identity theft).

- **Higher cost:** An average laptop with middle-of-the-road features often costs more than $1,000. A high-end, powerful laptop often costs $2,000 or more.

- **Less versatile:** The average laptop is limited to activities that fall under the light general-use category. However, expensive top-of-the-line laptops often have just as much power as most desktop PCs.

- **Limited upgrades:** A laptop cannot be opened to have its internal components replaced or upgraded. Instead, you have to add external upgrades such as cards that fit into the special slots on the side of the laptop, or external devices such as a hard drive or rewritable DVD drive that connects to the laptop's USB or FireWire ports.

Figure 16-2: Typical notebook

Note

Purchasing a laptop doesn't mean you can't use it at your home or office in the same way you would use a desktop. Special "base stations" allow you to connect a laptop to a normal desktop monitor, and nearly all laptops allow you to connect a regular, full-sized keyboard and mouse to them.

Features

Once you have selected a computer type and chosen a style, your next step is to figure out which features you want. Here is a list of the four computer types and the hardware they typically offer:

Light General Use

- Slower processor (CPU): Up to 1.8 GHz
- Limited amount of system memory (RAM): Up to 256MB
- Smaller hard drive: Between 40 and 80GB

Heavy General Use

- Medium-speed processor (CPU): Approximately 2.4 GHz
- Average amount of system memory (RAM): Between 512 and 1024MB
- Large hard drive: 80GB or more

Gaming

- Fast processor (CPU): 2.6 GHz or more
- Large amount of system memory (RAM): Minimum of 1024MB
- Large hard drive: 80GB or more
- High-end speakers with a subwoofer or a complete surround-sound system
- Powerful video card containing more than 128MB of video memory

High Performance

- Fast processor (CPU): 2.8 GHz or more
- Large amount of system memory (RAM): Minimum of 1024MB
- Extra-large hard drive: Minimum of 100GB
- Recordable or rewritable DVD drive

Warranty

Have you noticed that when you buy a piece of equipment from a computer or electronics store, the salespeople immediately pounce on you and ask you to buy an extended warranty or service plan?

Although that approach is extremely annoying, it doesn't mean that warranties should be avoided. Usually, it doesn't make sense to buy a warranty for an inexpensive product, but a warranty might be a wise decision for purchases that cost $1,000 or more. Before you buy any warranty, you should always examine its features such as the length of coverage and the things it won't cover (which are usually listed in the fine print, so take the time to read it). Here are several things a good service plan should include:

- **No lemon policy:** If the product needs a certain number of repairs within a specified time limit, you will receive a new version of that product (or its equivalent). For example, if your laptop has to be repaired more than three times in one year, most warranties will replace that laptop with a new one.

- **Battery coverage:** If the product's battery stops working properly, it will be repaired or replaced.

- **Power-surge protection:** If the product is damaged as a result of a power surge through your electrical outlets, it will be repaired or replaced. This can be quite valuable if you live or work in an area that has unreliable electricity. But be warned: Some warranties specifically indicate that they do not cover damage caused by power surges entering a computer through other sources such as telephone wires connected to the computer's dial-up modem.

- **Renewable:** When your original warranty expires, you can renew or extend it for a specified amount of time.

- **Transferable:** The warranty stays with the product, not with the person who bought it. That means if you sell or donate your product to someone else, the warranty can still be used by that person.

INDEX

INDEX

INDEX

Continued

Continued